M000267467

# Mindfulness Meditation
# Made Simple

# Mindfulness Meditation Made Simple

## Your Guide to Finding True Inner Peace

### Charles A. Francis

**P**P

Paradigm Press
Raleigh, NC

Paradigm Press
P.O. Box 12432
Raleigh, NC 27605
www.ParadigmPress.org

Copyright © 2015 by Charles A. Francis

All rights reserved. No part of this publication may be reproduced, distributed, or transmitted in any form or by any means, including photocopying, recording, or other electronic or mechanical methods, without the prior written permission of the publisher, except in the case of brief quotations embodied in critical reviews and certain other noncommercial uses permitted by copyright law. For permission requests, write to the publisher.

Quantity Orders:
Special discounts are available on quantity purchases by corporations, associations, and others. U.S. trade bookstores and wholesalers also receive special discounts. For details, contact the publisher at www.ParadigmPress.org.

Limit of Liability/Disclaimer of Warranty: Although the author and publisher have made every effort to ensure that the information in this book was correct at press time, the author and publisher do not assume and hereby disclaim any liability to any party for any loss, damage, or disruption caused by errors or omissions, whether such errors or omissions result from negligence, accident, or any other cause. This book is not intended as a substitute for the medical advice of physicians. The reader should regularly consult a physician in matters relating to his/her health and particularly with respect to any symptoms that may require diagnosis or medical attention.

Publisher's Cataloging-In-Publication Data

Francis, Charles A., 1961-
   Mindfulness meditation made simple : your guide to finding true inner peace / Charles A. Francis.

    pages ;  cm

    Includes index.
    Issued also as an ebook.
    ISBN: 978-0-9908405-0-3

   1. Meditation. 2. Awareness. 3. Attention. 4. Peace of mind. 5. Meditations. I. Title.

BF637.M4 F73 2014
158.12                                                          2014952203

This book is printed on environmentally friendly acid-free paper. It is printed on 30% PCW recycled paper. The interior paper is supplied by an FSC-certified provider.

Cover and interior design by: Cornelia Georgiana Murariu

Printed in the United States of America

This book is dedicated to my mom,
who has always been there for me,
and who taught me that in life,
failure is not an option.

∼

To my soulmate, Mary, who has brought so
much love and joy into my life.

∼

And to all my readers, may you find the
peace and happiness you're searching for.

## About the Author

 Charles A. Francis is the cofounder and director of the Mindfulness Meditation Institute. He has studied the practice of mindfulness with Zen master Thich Nhat Hanh. For over 18 years, he has worked to help people find inner peace through mindfulness meditation.

Charles has published numerous articles, and is the author of the ebook, Mindfulness in the Workplace: How Organizations Are Using Mindfulness to Lower Health Care Cost and Increase Productivity.

Charles has a master's degree in Public Administration from Syracuse University, with a focus on health care management and policy. He has worked for the North Carolina State Senate in writing legislation to address childhood obesity, and government efficiency. He has a background in accounting and business management, and has served as CEO of ITC, an international telecommunications company.

He also earned a master's degree in International Relations while studying in China and Japan. There he studied various facets of Asian culture, such as society, history, economics, and politics. He also studied both the Chinese and Japanese languages.

Charles has conducted research in systems evolution, and has identified the key principles by which systems evolve. These principles apply to all types of systems, such as organizational, social, economic, and biological systems. They have significant implications regarding how organizations develop and are managed, how public policy is structured, and how humans evolve physically and consciously.

Charles helps organizations develop mindfulness training programs, in order to help them realize the cost-saving benefits of the mindfulness practice. He also leads workshops and mindfulness retreats. He is available for consulting and speaking engagements. You can contact him at Charles@MindfulnessMeditationInstitute.org.

## How to Contact the Author

Charles Francis is available for mindfulness consulting for businesses, associations, nonprofit organizations, and government institutions. Requests for further information, availability for speaking, and consulting should be directed to the address and phone number below:

The Mindfulness Meditation Institute
P.O. Box 12432
Raleigh, NC 27605

Phone: (919) 803-3517
Email: Charles@MindfulnessMeditationInstitute.org

Web site: www.MindfulnessMeditationInstitute.org
Facebook: www.facebook.com/MindfulnessMeditationInstitute
Twitter: @CharlesAFrancis
Twitter: @TrainingMindful
Linkedin: www.linkedin.com/pub/charles-a-francis/49/7b2/b09

Attention colleges, universities, corporations, government and nonprofit organizations: Quantity discounts are available for bulk purchases of this book. The book may be used for training, fundraising, or gift-giving purposes. For more information, please visit the publisher's web site: www.ParadigmPress.org.

## What Other Authors Are Saying about
*"Mindfulness Meditation Made Simple"*

"From his own experience, Charles Francis has developed a 12 step program for establishing a mindfulness meditation practice. *Mindfulness Meditation Made Simple* will be welcomed by recovery communities of all types. In a hands-on style, this book effectively cuts through common obstacles to the practice."—Sharon Salzberg, co-founder of the Insight Meditation Society, and author of *Real Happiness*

"In *Mindfulness Meditation Made Simple,* Charles Francis has given his readers valuable practical guidance on mindfulness meditation. It will help beginners gain a solid foundation of the practice. He engages his readers in lively discussion on mindfulness and clear comprehension. It is an invaluable book."—Bhante Henepola Gunaratana, author of *Mindfulness in Plain English,* and several other books on meditation

"Simple, direct, and practical, Charles Francis lays out an effective path to making mindfulness a part of your life, and a catalyst to greater personal ease, peace, and happiness."—Elisha Goldstein, PhD, author of *Uncovering Happiness: Overcoming Depression with Mindfulness and Self-Compassion,* and coauthor of *A Mindfulness-Based Stress Reduction Workbook*

"You may have read the cover story in Time magazine, or heard about world class athletes and celebrities extolling the virtues of mindfulness meditation. Modern science is now catching up with the subjective experiences that meditators have had for thousands of years. In his book, Charles Francis teaches in simple and elegant terms how you can be more creative, happier, and find fulfillment by practicing mindfulness meditation."—Sanjiv Chopra, MD, Professor of Medicine at Harvard Medical School, author, and motivational speaker

"The ancient practice of mindfulness meditation is comprehensively explained in *Mindfulness Meditation Made Simple,* for the beginner, experienced student, and anyone wishing to incorporate mindfulness into his or her life in a thorough, illuminating, and practical way."—Diana Winston, Director of Mindfulness Education at UCLA's Mindful Awareness Research Center, and coauthor of *Fully Present: The Science, Art, and Practice of Mindfulness*

"In *Mindfulness Meditation Made Simple,* Charles Francis offers us a roadmap from the surface of life to our center where a life worth living begins. With mindfulness, we remember that while we must live on the surface of life and exist in a human skin, the presence of the One is always with us, every moment, one step, one breath, one sacred second at a time.

Living closer to the center of our being is the practice of a lifetime, but so, too, is skillfully living on the horizontal plane—the surface of life. This book will guide you to that sacred intersection where your Being commingles with your doing in the most amazing ways! Read this book as the first in your mindfulness practice—it will change your life."—Dennis Merritt Jones, award-winning author of *Your Redefining Moments: Becoming Who You Were Born to Be,* and *The Art of Uncertainty: How to Live in the Mystery of Life and Love It*

"*Mindfulness Meditation Made Simple* shows anyone the keys to finding long-lasting happiness by eliminating the sources of suffering within. With its practices, anyone can achieve more loving and fulfilling relationships. It is a blueprint for inner peace and serenity."—Sarah McLean, best-selling author of *Soul-Centered: Transform Your Life in 8 Weeks with Meditation*

"I appreciate the way that Charles Francis has drawn from his personal experience to write the 12 Steps of Mindfulness Meditation Practice. In particular, I recommend his advice for practicing deep listening, mindful speech, and a forgiving approach to relationships."—Susan Gillis Chapman, author of *The Five Keys To Mindful Communication*

"Mindfulness meditation has extensive, well-researched benefits, and Charles Francis has created a clear, progressive, 12-step guide for learning and applying the practice. *Mindfulness Meditation Made Simple* is a helpful resource to get you started and keep you on track." —Stephan Bodian, author of *Meditation for Dummies,* and the Mindfulness Meditation mobile program

"Charles Francis' *Mindfulness Meditation Made Simple* is an incredibly helpful resource that provides easy to implement guidance to those who are just beginning a mindfulness meditation practice, as well as to those looking to expand and deepen their existing practice. In 12 simple, concise steps Francis teaches the basics of the mindfulness meditation practice, gives guidance on enhancing more advanced practice, addresses eliminating obstacles to spiritual growth (the five hindrances), provides direction for writing meditation, and encourages teaching others.

As a mindfulness practitioner and teacher myself, I love how this book not only gently nudges you toward a more mindful approach to living in all areas of your life, but also gives you the skills to heal past wounds, deepen your relationships, eliminate suffering, and achieve an amazing feeling of inner peace.

You will understand how the Three Jewels from Buddhism can speed up your spiritual evolution, and you will have everything you need to create or participate in a meditation group to enhance your practice. Plus, the expertly designed exercises at the end of each chapter will guide and quicken your progress to help you truly transform your life."—Debra Burdick, LCSWR, BCN, author of *Mindfulness Skills Workbook for Clinicians and Clients: 111 Tools, Techniques, Activities and Worksheets.* www.TheBrainLady.com

"In *Mindfulness Meditation Made Simple,* Charles Francis shows us how to realize our full potential through the practice of mindfulness meditation. This books distills the essence of mindfulness meditation with clarity and skill, offering these perennial wisdom teachings in a universally accessible way. I highly recommend this book."—Shauna Shapiro, PhD, coauthor of *Mindful Discipline: A Loving Approach to Setting Limits and Raising an Emotionally Intelligent Child,* and *The Art and Science of Mindfulness*

"*Mindfulness Meditation Made Simple* is great for both beginning and experienced meditators. Charles Francis draws on his own profound experiences and insights to show beginners how to get off to a great start, and then how to get the most from your meditation practice. I recommend it to anyone serious about meditation."—Dr. Ian Gawler, OAM, author of *The Mind that Changes Everything,* and *Meditation: An In-Depth Guide*

"*Mindfulness Meditation Made Simple* is a practical book to learn mindfulness meditation. Charles Francis gives you the essential meditation tools for finding more balance, joy, and peace in your life."—Bob Stahl, PhD, coauthor of *A Mindfulness-Based Stress Reduction Workbook, Living With Your Heart Wide Open, Calming the Rush of Panic,* and *A Mindfulness-Based Stress Reduction Workbook for Anxiety*

"Here is a simple but in-depth set of tools for practicing mindfulness both in meditation and in daily life. Charles shows us step-by-step how Buddhism and mindfulness contribute to our becoming psychologically and spiritually healthy."—David Richo, author of *How to Be an Adult in Love: Letting Love in Safely and Showing It Recklessly* (Shambhala, 2013)

"This book provides a great introduction to and overview of mindfulness practices that anyone with the desire to enhance his or her life can easily use."—Sandra Waddock, author of *Intellectual Shamans: Management Academics Making a Difference,* Cambridge, in press.

# Contents

# PART I
## THE BASICS OF YOUR MINDFULNESS MEDITATION PRACTICE

# PART II
## HOW TO ENHANCE YOUR PRACTICE

# PART III

## ELIMINATE THE OBSTACLES TO YOUR SPIRITUAL GROWTH

# PART IV

## CARRYING THE MESSAGE

# Foreword

According to the World Health Organization, stress has become the leading health problem in the United States. The American Medical Association says it is a factor in more than 75 percent of all illnesses today. However, Americans aren't the only ones with a stress problem. Stress has also become a worldwide epidemic, and it is robbing us of our peace and harmony.

Stress is a normal part of being human, but too much of it is not good for us. When we're under too much stress, we are not at peace. We can feel anxious, fearful, and it can feel like we're losing control of our lives, which can lead to strained relations with loved ones. Furthermore, stress can lead to various health problems, such as depression, high blood pressure, heart disease, stroke, and many others. How we deal with stress determines whether we suffer the consequences. Fortunately, there is a simple solution: the practice of mindfulness meditation.

In recent years, people all over the world have become increasingly interested in mindfulness meditation. I am encouraged to see them becoming so enthusiastic, and eager to begin meditating. People of different spiritual faiths are realizing that mindfulness meditation is a practice, and not a religion. So, it is compatible with just about any faith.

A great deal of research has confirmed many of the health benefits of the practice, especially stress reduction. And better health means less health care expenses and physical suffering. But most importantly, mindfulness meditation will help you find inner peace, or freedom from suffering, which is what the Buddha originally intended.

In his new book, *Mindfulness Meditation Made Simple*, Charles Francis shares with you the basics of the mindfulness meditation practice, so you can get started quickly. His unique 12-step approach shows you exactly what to do, and how to do it. He explains the concepts and techniques in clear and simple terms, so that a beginner will have no trouble following them, and begin achieving a noticeable personal transformation.

The book takes you even further. It shows you how to heal the wounds from your past, so you can be free of the pain and suffering they bring. It also covers other sources of stress, and explains how to use the practice to overcome them. And if you're a serious spiritual seeker, it shows you how to make mindfulness a way of life, and not just a practice.

One part of the book I really enjoyed was his discussion of mindful consumption. He explains interconnectedness from a scientific perspective. He uses an emerging field of study called systems evolution. He points out how unmindful consumption contributes to social, economic, and political tensions within and among societies, and how each of us can contribute to the easing of these tensions. But don't worry, he uses layman terms and relates the subject to everyday events in our lives, so we can learn to be more mindful of our consumption of limited resources.

Mindful consumption is important for various reasons. On a personal level, it will help us achieve better health, and to live within our means. On a global scale, mindful consumption will help us protect the environment and natural resources, which are often the sources of political and economic tensions.

Mindful consumption will also help businesses, government, and nonprofit organizations. It will enable them to operate more efficiently and effectively. Not only will it help them lower their health care expenses, but it will also help them become better stewards of their communities.

I also like the writing meditation technique Charles developed. This is an innovative way of learning the time-tested practice of loving-kindness that the Buddha originally taught. For those of you who are not familiar with loving-kindness meditation, it is a set of positive affirmations that helps us change our attitudes about ourselves, and other people. It helps us develop compassion for all living beings, which I believe is so important for our own happiness, and that of others.

Traditionally, the loving-kindness meditation was read or recited in order to assimilate these wholesome affirmations. With the writing meditation, Charles has combined the loving-kindness meditation with writing techniques to make the practice even more effective. I can see how this writing meditation can enhance your development of compassion, as studies have shown that writing can have a significant impact in changing our attitudes and behavior.

As you read the book, it becomes clear that Charles has many years of experience with mindfulness. After all, it takes a good understanding of a subject to be able to explain it clearly. He certainly learned well from Zen master Thich Nhat Hanh.

One of the things I like about the book is that he relates his own learning experiences as he explains various topics. By the time you finish reading it, not only do you understand the practice of mindfulness meditation, but you also feel like you know Charles on a personal level, and the challenges he encountered learning the practice. His unique approach to teaching mindfulness meditation is refreshing.

I am happy to see that Charles has developed a clear and simple method for learning mindfulness meditation. It will save you a lot of time and effort in trying to figure out how to meditate on your own. If you're a beginner, *Mindfulness Meditation Made Simple* will give you a solid foundation of the practice, and have you making immediate and steady progress in your spiritual development. It has everything you need to get started, and to keep you moving forward.

Cultivating mindfulness is essential if you want to learn how to overcome stress, and achieve long-lasting peace and serenity. Your relationships will improve, because you'll eliminate the mental agitation that is keeping you from being fully present when you're with loved ones. In addition, you'll become more loving and compassionate, which will improve your interactions and relationships with everyone you meet. Mindfulness will truly enrich your life.

Lower stress will also lead to better health. You will feel much better physically, and avoid many medical expenses. Mindfulness will enable you to see more clearly the consequences of your actions, and empower you to make better choices in all areas of your life.

The book is also for the serious spiritual seeker who wants to take his spiritual development to a higher level. As mindfulness becomes a way of life for you, all your thoughts and actions will come in line with the spiritual principles that govern the universe, which will further enhance your development of mindfulness, and bring you closer to nirvana.

This book has come at an important time in history. Mindfulness is not a fad, but rather a movement whose time has finally come, and you are a vital part of this movement. With the growing interest in mindfulness worldwide, people need a simple and straightforward manner of learning the practice. I think *Mindfulness Meditation Made Simple* fulfills this need, and it will make a significant contribution to helping cultivate peace and harmony in the world. It is a must-read for anyone who is serious about meditation, and wants to help bring about world peace.

Bhante Henepola Gunaratana
Author of *Mindfulness in Plain English*

# Preface

As you probably know, mindfulness meditation has become quite popular in recent years. There are several reasons for this: (1) prominent figures spreading the practice, (2) scientific research confirming its benefits, and (3) the practice is compatible with Western values, and other spiritual faiths. But the main reason for its popularity is that people who engage in the practice see results, and quickly. Mindfulness meditation has gone from obscurity to mainstream.

Today, mindfulness is being applied in almost all areas of society, such as health care, business, education, the military, mental health, and even politics. Mindfulness is transforming our lives in ways we never imagined. And all this is happening in an age of multitasking and fast-paced everything.

My journey in learning how to meditate was not an easy one. Back in 1996 when I first began, there were very few books that explained the practice clearly. Much of my learning was through trial and error, and deciphering the books that were available at the time. Today, we are fortunate to have many good books and articles available to help us in our practice.

So in order to make it easier for beginners, I took what I knew about Buddhism and meditation and formatted it in a way that was easy to understand, and put into practice. My goal was to save you the years of frustration that I experienced learning how to meditate.

This book is for the spiritual seeker who is serious about personal transformation. I take the same approach as the Buddha: I give you the tools for realizing freedom from your suffering. I try not to preach a doctrine, but rather show you how to see the nature of your existence for yourself, so you can find true inner peace. So, the book's main focus is the practice.

When I first started writing this book, I had no intention of writing one. I was actually writing the script for a DVD on meditation. Then one day I realized that I had almost enough material for a book, so I decided to reformat the material into 12 simple steps with exercises to help spiritual seekers learn the practice. Most of my time was spent rewriting and editing. I wanted to make the instructions as clear and straightforward as possible. I also wanted to make it enjoyable, so that seekers would remain motivated and enthusiastic, which are a couple of the biggest challenges for beginners.

Overall, it took about 3 ½ years to complete the book. I would have finished it sooner, but I got a bit sidetracked in 2013. My life partner, Mary Sovran, was diagnosed with esophageal cancer. Fortunately, doctors found the cancer in the early stages. She underwent chemotherapy, radiation treatment, and major surgery that year. Though I was still able to work on the book, my priority was to help her in her recovery. I am happy to say that she is doing very well now, and so far, she is cancer free.

The purpose of *Mindfulness Meditation Made Simple* is to give beginners a solid foundation of the practice, and to help experienced practitioners get more from their efforts. The 12 Steps of the Mindfulness Meditation Practice are designed to teach you the basic principles of the practice, show you how to implement them in your life, and to take your spirituality to a higher level. This new approach will help you find the peace and happiness you're searching for, and to discover your true potential.

As you progress in your practice, you'll find that mindfulness meditation will enrich your life. It will improve your health, relationships, and your mental abilities, including memory. This will help you lower your health care expenses, and make you more productive in everything you do. And surely, researchers will find new ways that it can improve the quality of our lives, and our society as well. Mindfulness will empower you to pursue the life of your dreams, and to help make the world a better place.

*Mindfulness Meditation Made Simple* is the kind of book that should be studied, and not simply read. You will transform your life only by putting the principles into practice. What I would suggest is that you start a meditation group with your friends, so you can study and practice the 12 Steps of the Mindfulness Meditation Practice together. A meditation group will give you the support vital to your spiritual growth.

To help you get started, I've developed a group starter kit that supplies you with guidelines, a sample format, and literature to make the process easy for you. You can download the kit from our website (http://www.MindfulnessMeditationInstitute.org/resources). There is no charge for the kit.

As you begin to reach a higher level of spiritual awakening, your concern for the well-being of others will deepen, and the practice will help you in your service to mankind. It is my sincere hope that you will take these 12 steps to heart, and use them to not only transform your own life, but also our society. My vision is to see a vast network of groups practicing and teaching the 12 Steps, so that we take mankind to the next level of his evolutionary path.

There are several people throughout my life who have helped and inspired me on my spiritual journey. The first is my mother, who showed me by raising four children on her own that failure is not an option. Stephen Ringer, my first mentor, taught me the importance of taking personal responsibility for my healing and spiritual development. Jeff Gustafson has been a good friend and confidant, who helps ensure that my reasoning is sound: and those who have taught me much of what I know about mindfulness, Thich Nhat Hanh and Bhante Gunaratana. To all, I am truly grateful.

I owe a special thanks to Mary, who has been so helpful, supportive, and patient during the writing of this book. Her insightful suggestions have made this a better book for you.

# INTRODUCTION

*Greater than the tread of mighty armies*
*is an idea whose time has come.*

~ VICTOR HUGO

## Chapter Highlights

- Why All the Confusion?
- What Is Mindfulness Meditation?
- Why Practice Mindfulness Meditation?
- The 12 Steps of the Mindfulness
  Meditation Practice
- How to Use This Book
- How to Stay Focused and Committed
  to Your Practice
- The Courage to Change
- Exercises for Getting Started

WE ARE AT A CRITICAL POINT in history, where two opposing trends are influencing the direction of mankind, trends that will determine the course of evolution in human consciousness. On the one hand, people are caught up in an ever increasing fast-paced life, fueled by advances in technology designed to help make their lives easier, and more meaningful. And on the other hand, some are on a spiritual quest to help them find relief from the pressures of daily life, and to understand the true nature of their existence. Both trends are intended to bring order out of chaos, but while some are searching for happiness, others are in search of true inner peace.

Over the last few years, interest in mindfulness meditation has surged. Almost every week, I hear about innovative ways people are using the practice in everyday life, not just to deal with physical and psychological problems, but also to help them reach their highest potential.

Mindfulness meditation is becoming so widely accepted that it is now being taught in schools, corporations, and in government. Even celebrities, such as Oprah Winfrey and Arianna Huffington, are promoting the practice. All indications are that this trend is only going to continue. We are in the midst of a revolution—the Mindfulness Revolution.

One of the reasons mindfulness meditation has become so popular is that scientists have been conducting a tremendous amount of research on the practice. They are confirming the benefits that practitioners have advocated for many years, and they're continuing to make breakthroughs every day.

Researchers have discovered that mindfulness meditation helps people overcome many health problems, such as stress, high blood pressure, heart disease, substance abuse, depression, PTSD, and much more. It even slows the aging process, and helps people prevent chronic illnesses, which cost millions of dollars in health care—not to mention all the pain and suffering. This is particularly relevant in a time when health care costs are spiraling out of control.

Researchers have also found that the practice helps people enhance their mental capabilities, such as abstract thinking, memory, and creativity. It even helps people improve their leadership and social skills. Organizations are now including mindfulness training in their leadership training programs, as well as their health and wellness programs. This will create a new generation of more mindful leaders in both the public and private sectors.

Recent studies have shown that mindfulness meditation improves workplace productivity, in addition to lowering health care costs. This is good news for private organizations that want to increase profitability, while at the same time being responsible stewards of their community and the environment. It is also good news for public organizations that want to increase government efficiency, and make better use of taxpayer dollars.

Mindfulness meditation has been around for over 2,500 years, and it has proven itself in the lives of millions of people as an effective vehicle for achieving freedom from their suffering, and realizing true inner peace. However, it has been only recently that Westerners have become interested in the practice. Today, conditions are just right for the practice to become widely accepted in the West:

- **Changes in the social and political environment.** During the Cold War, there was a great deal of mistrust between Eastern and Western societies. The end of the Cold War has enabled more interaction between these cultures.

- **Advances in communication technology.** The rise of the Internet and other communication technologies have made communication between cultures much easier.

- **Prominent figures active in diffusing the practice.** Most notably, the Dalai Lama and Zen master Thich Nhat Hanh have been quite active in engaging the West. Interestingly, much of the Dalai Lama's interaction has been with the scientific community, to encourage scientists to conduct research on the practice.

- **Compatibility with Western values.** Since mindfulness meditation is a practice, and not a religion, practitioners don't have to abandon their current spiritual faith in order to avail themselves of the benefits of the practice.

- **Effectiveness of the practice.** Mindfulness meditation is proving to be extremely effective for all-around personal development, as well as health improvement. Practitioners are finding that the practice enables them to function at optimal levels physically, mentally, and emotionally.

There is also a growing trend toward non-religious forms of spirituality. In recent years, we've seen a growing number of Americans identifying themselves as spiritual but not religious. Many of them are no longer satisfied with accepting a predetermined spiritual doctrine, and want to search for the truth for themselves. Mindfulness meditation is an ideal alternative for these spiritual seekers.

While it is encouraging that more people are interested in mindfulness meditation, there is still a great deal of confusion about the practice. Meditation is a foreign concept to many people, and there are many misconceptions about it, so beginners are often unsure about how to get started in their practice.

Unless you have a straightforward manner of learning the practice, it will take you several years to learn effective meditation techniques, and make significant progress in your spiritual development. This is one of the main reasons why many people simply give up before they realize any results. I learned the hard way, but you don't have to.

Meditation isn't as complicated as you might think, and this book presents the mindfulness meditation practice in a manner that is easy to understand, so you can implement the techniques and begin making noticeable progress immediately. I have developed an easy-to-follow twelve-step approach to learning mindfulness meditation that will give you a solid foundation of the practice as quickly as possible. This new approach will save you years of effort trying to figure it out on your own, like I did. You'll see for yourself that it's a myth that it takes years of meditation to find inner peace.

While there are indeed many benefits to the practice, the Buddha's original goal was to put an end to human suffering. Through mindful leadership, we can help others achieve freedom from their suffering. But in order for us to be effective, we must be an example for others to follow. Therefore, the primary focus of this book will be on how to achieve freedom from our own suffering through personal transformation. We'll begin by examining some of the common problems people encounter early in their meditation practice.

## Why All the Confusion?

I had such a hard time learning how to meditate when I first started. Each time I asked someone how to do it, I got a different answer, and a vague one at that. I was confused for a long time, but didn't want to admit it. Years later, I realized that I wasn't the only one having a hard time.

The main reason for the confusion about meditation is that there are many different forms of meditation, and too many choices lead to confusion. When confronted with too many choices, we either try as many as we can, or none at all. Either way, we get nowhere.

If we're always trying different forms of meditation, we never become proficient with any of them. It's like trying to learn to play a different musical instrument every week. You'll never learn to play music that way, so why would you expect to learn how to meditate using the same approach? Doesn't it makes more sense to choose a well-established form of meditation, and practice it until you become proficient with it? Then you'll have a basis for evaluating other forms.

## What Is Mindfulness Meditation?

Mindfulness meditation is a secular form of meditation that has its roots in Vipassana, the oldest form of meditation the Buddha originally taught over 2,500 years ago. The main goal is to attain freedom from suffering. You see, our suffering is the result of our unwholesome emotions, thoughts, and actions, which are triggered by our inaccurate views of the world and ourselves. Through mindfulness meditation, we can develop greater awareness, or mindfulness, which will enable us to make better decisions in our life. In other words, mindfulness meditation is the practice that leads to the development of mindfulness.

> *"We can never obtain peace in the outer world until we make peace with ourselves."*
>
> – DALAI LAMA

When we were growing up, many of us learned that to achieve happiness, we had to indulge in pleasant emotions and avoid unpleasant emotions—sometimes at any cost—and that cost was often at other people's expense. So we often ended up compromising the harmony within ourselves, and with the people around us.

Our cultures usually tell us how to find happiness. In Western societies, we learn to find happiness and fulfillment through a successful career, marriage, children, and material belongings. This is the American dream. So we spend our whole lives chasing after these things, and some of them do bring us joy, such as our spouse and our children. But there are a couple of problems with depending on these things to bring us happiness:

**We have no control over things outside of us.** Many of the sources of our happiness are outside of us and beyond our control, and we often have difficulty accepting this fact. So when we don't get our way, we sometimes become angry and frightened. Then we become controlling and manipulative in order to keep from losing our cherished possessions. We can also become overwhelmed and stressed out when it seems like we're losing control.

**All things are impermanent.** Many of us have the illusion that we'll live happily ever after, once we get all the things we want. We think that our lives will then be complete. But when we finally reach that point, we begin to worry about them slipping away. Do you ever worry about losing your job, your wealth, or your good health? Sure you do. We worry because life has an uncanny way of forcing the truth on us—that all of these things are impermanent.

> Just as an athlete trains his body, a meditator trains his mind.

So how can we find happiness when all the things we cherish will one day be gone? The answer is to look for happiness within ourselves. By looking within, we'll begin to see that we're much more than we think. We'll see that we're connected with a consciousness much greater than our own. In other words, we're not alone in this world—and this is a tremendous comfort.

With mindfulness meditation, you'll develop an awareness of the true nature of reality. By observing what is happening within your mind, body, and the world around you, you'll begin to lift the veil of illusion that creates the suffering in your life. This is essentially what a spiritual awakening is.

The foundation of your practice will be the development of concentration and mindfulness. These are your primary tools of observation. By developing them, you'll be able to look deeply into the true nature of reality. The 12 Steps of the Mindfulness Meditation Practice outlined in this book will guide you through the process step-by-step.

## Why Practice Mindfulness Meditation?

As I mentioned above, the ultimate goal of practicing mindfulness meditation is to attain freedom from our suffering, or inner peace. Now that may sound rather abstract, so it might be a good idea to talk about how your life will change through the practice.

Probably the best way to illustrate what mindfulness meditation can do for you is to share my own experience with the practice. When I was in my early 20s, I was a very frightened young man. I was afraid of just about everyone and everything.

I was afraid to talk to people because my self-esteem was so low that I couldn't see why people would waste their time talking to me. I felt I had nothing to offer them. I thought I was dull and uninteresting. The sad irony was that I probably was. As a result, I was unable to form meaningful relationships.

I started on a spiritual path by reading books about spirituality, and getting involved in different groups where we'd talk about applying spiritual principles to our lives. Some of the people in the groups practiced meditation, but I had no idea what it was about, or how to practice it. I intuitively discovered that I could relieve stress by going to the park and sitting quietly and contemplating the things that were happening in my life. This also helped me stay motivated in following a spiritual path.

After about 11 years of practicing this way, I felt like I needed something more. I had always been skeptical about the existence of a Supreme Being, but I was caught in the difficult position of wanting to attain a higher level of spirituality and not knowing how to reach it. Many of the people I was practicing with eventually reached a plateau, and most of them were content with it. But, I wasn't.

One spring day in 1996, as I sat quietly at my desk at home contemplating the direction of my life, I slipped into what seemed like an altered state of consciousness. I had the distinct feeling that time had come to a complete stop, and I was seeing the essence of who I really was.

When I came back to normal consciousness, everything looked surreal and I felt an incredible peace that I had never felt before, as if all my troubles had simply vanished. Suddenly, I could see everything clearly. My entire life now made complete sense. I realized that even though I felt lost much of my life, I was never lost at all. Instead, all my pain and suffering had served an important purpose. The confusion was gone.

I also felt wide awake, as if I had been asleep my whole life. I now had an awareness, or a sense, that I didn't have before. I began to understand the true nature of my suffering, especially how deeply it penetrated my psyche.

I realized that the root cause of my suffering had been just plain ignorance, or unmindfulness. Since I didn't understand how the world worked, I unknowingly created my own suffering by making poor decisions. But now, with my ability to see more clearly, it became possible to overcome my suffering. Then it became apparent that the way I had found this inner peace was by following a spiritual path.

After this experience, I began to learn more about meditation. It was a slow process because I didn't know anyone who understood it well enough to teach me. I read several books on meditation, but could never really understand how to implement the practice. It took me years to figure out what worked, and what didn't.

I tried various forms of meditation over the next few years. The main problem I encountered was trying to stay awake, and nobody ever taught me how to deal with this problem—or any other problems, such as a racing mind. Then I tried mindfulness meditation, and was absolutely amazed at how well it worked. I began to grow once again, and the results were immediate and profound.

What I liked about mindfulness meditation was that it gave me some very powerful tools—something I didn't find in other forms of meditation. I could adapt the practice to my changing needs as I continued growing. The main reason I now practice mindfulness meditation exclusively is that it really works, and I continue to see results. Mindfulness meditation helped speed up my development significantly. Here is a small sample of what my life is like today:

- I have a self-confidence that is unshakable.
- I rarely get angry.
- Fear has dissipated significantly.

- I am no longer haunted by painful memories of the past.
- Difficult situations no longer cause me stress or anxiety.
- My relationships with people have improved tremendously.
- Even my mental abilities have improved—including memory.

The one change in my life that I'm probably the most grateful for is that I never feel lonely. When I was young, loneliness was the predominant emotion in my life. Today, I am free from all that pain and suffering.

These are just some of the changes I've gone through, which you too can expect. Imagine the possibilities. Mindfulness meditation will change your life in countless ways:

- **Tap into your inner strength.** Without your fears holding you back, you'll unlock your true potential, so you can pursue your dreams like never before.

- **Unleash your creativity.** Even if you're not a creative person, you'll be amazed at how the practice will stimulate your creativity. You'll discover many hidden talents.

- **Reprogram your subconscious.** You will finally overcome stubborn habits, such as smoking and overeating. The practice will help you reach your ideal weight.

- **Look and feel younger.** Research has shown that mindfulness meditation slows the aging process. People who meditate regularly tend to look and feel much younger than their actual age.

- **Improve your health.** Hundreds of studies in recent years have confirmed that mindfulness meditation has a wide range of health benefits, such as stress reduction, lower blood pressure, decreased risk of heart disease, overcoming depression and substance abuse, improved immune system, pain management, and many more.

As scientists continue making breakthroughs in mindfulness research, they're finding that mindfulness meditation can improve just about every area of our lives. In essence, the practice will help you discover a new you, and the great news is that you'll achieve results in just a week or two of practice. Others will see a tremendous difference in you.

## The 12 Steps of the Mindfulness Meditation Practice

The 12 Steps of the Mindfulness Meditation Practice is a unique approach that I developed especially for you, the spiritual seeker, to help you learn the practice as quickly as possible—while helping you avoid the pitfalls. It gives beginning and experienced practitioners a step-by-step format that is easy to follow—and if you have the *Quick Start to Mindfulness Meditation* CD, you'll have a couple of ready-made meditations you can follow.

> Mindfulness meditation is a practice, and not a religion, so it is compatible with most spiritual traditions.

You'll learn the basic techniques so you can begin practicing right away. They will also take you to an intermediate level, so you can speed up your development even more. With this new approach, you will:

- Develop a solid foundation of the mindfulness meditation practice.
- Find out how to avoid the most common pitfalls.
- Save time and effort.
- Achieve immediate and noticeable results.

When you learn to practice mindfulness meditation using this approach, you will achieve an inner peace that you never imagined possible. And since mindfulness meditation is a practice, and not a religion, it is compatible with most other spiritual traditions.

Most of us had our beginnings in a particular spiritual tradition for good reasons, so you don't need to abandon your Christian, Jewish, Muslim, or other faith. In fact, most spiritual traditions incorporate meditation into their practice. Mindfulness meditation will actually help you gain a much deeper understanding of your current spiritual faith.

The benefits that meditation has to offer are almost limitless, for those who are willing to put in the effort. By dwelling in the three main sources of spiritual nourishment: our True Nature, the spiritual principles, and our spiritual community,

> *"The future begins today."*
> – WAYNE GERARD TROTMAN

we learn to live mindfully in the present moment. These are the steps we follow in order to achieve freedom from our suffering:

**Step 1—"We became aware of the pain and suffering created by unmindful thoughts, speech, and actions."** Step 1 teaches you some important concepts to help you understand the practice. In this step, we'll talk about the Four Noble Truths, which deal with suffering and how to overcome it. We will also talk about the Five Hindrances, which deal with things that get in the way of your meditation and spiritual development.

**Step 2—"We learned how to develop our primary tools of observation: concentration and mindfulness."** Here you will learn how to use your two most important tools of observation. If we want to understand ourselves, and our relationships with others, then we need to learn how to observe the world with unbiased clarity.

We often make quick judgments based on preconceived ideas, because it's easier than examining situations further, and often less painful in the short-run. That is, we jump to conclusions without having many of the facts. So, to observe reality without bias, we need to develop our skills of observation. Like a journalist, we're trying to get at the truth.

**Step 3—"We sought to eliminate the things that agitate our mind, and prevent us from achieving inner peace and serenity."** A common challenge for beginners is dealing with a racing mind. We're often unaware that many of our daily activities are agitating our mind. In this step, I'll show you how to identify and eliminate the sources of agitation. I'll also give you some effective tools for calming your mind.

**Step 4—"We learned how to structure our meditation session for maximum effectiveness, and to fit our lifestyle."** In Step 4, we discuss our meditation environment. There is no best time or place that applies to everyone, because we all have different commitments and living situations. I'll give you some guidelines for choosing the best time and place for you. We'll also talk about sitting position and how long to meditate.

**Step 5—"In order to enhance our spiritual evolution, we made mindfulness meditation a regular practice."** This step deals with the actual mechanics of meditation. You'll learn exactly what to do during your meditation sessions. I'll give you different formats, so you can choose the one that's most suitable for your needs, and I will even guide you through a typical meditation session.

**Step 6—"We remained vigilant in our meditation practice, so that we continued making steady progress."** In Step 6, you'll learn how to track your progress by keeping a meditation journal. This will help you stay grounded in proper techniques by establishing goals and measuring your progress. It will also help you stay motivated.

**Step 7—"We became aware that other people can provide us with the spiritual nourishment vital to our development."** Other people can be invaluable sources of spiritual nourishment that will dramatically speed up your development. I will show you how to connect with them, so that you not only enhance your own spiritual development, but also that of others.

**Step 8—"We sought to cultivate peace and harmony in our relationships and interactions with others by practicing deep listening, mindful speech, non-judging, and forgiveness."** In this step, we'll examine how our behavior impacts our spiritual development and our relationships, and I'll share with you some powerful tools for improving them.

**Step 9—"We sought to dwell deeply in our spiritual community in order to enhance our development, and that of others."** In Step 9, I'll show you how to avail yourself of the healing power of your spiritual community. I will introduce you to some more useful tools for enhancing your practice, including loving-kindness meditation, and a new meditation technique we've developed—writing

> The most powerful tool of our practice is the mindfulness meditation retreat

meditation. You will also learn about the most powerful tool of all—the mindfulness meditation retreat.

**Step 10—"We became aware of how unmindful consumption perpetuates our suffering, and prevents us from achieving true inner peace."** In this step, we'll discuss how your consumption of nutrients and other substances can either enhance or hinder your spiritual development. As you progress in your practice, you'll develop the wisdom and inner strength to make healthier choices.

**Step 11—"With the strength, courage, and mindfulness we attained through our meditation practice, we confronted and overcame the wounds from our past."** Many of us have wounds from long ago that have never healed. These are serious obstacles to our development. In Step 11, I will show you how to use your emerging mindfulness to overcome them, so you can be free of them once and for all.

**Step 12—"Having found freedom from our suffering through mindfulness meditation, we shared this practice with others, and continued dwelling deeply in the present moment through mindful living."** One of the great gifts you will receive from your practice is a deep sense of caring and compassion for other people. In this step, you'll learn how to help others achieve inner peace as you have, and how your mindful leadership can help create a more mindful society. You'll also learn how to apply mindfulness to all your daily activities, so that you continue making progress.

With these steps, you will learn: (1) the basic techniques of mindfulness meditation, (2) techniques for enhancing your practice, (3) how to eliminate obstacles that slow your progress, and (4) how teaching others the practice will benefit you, the student, and society as a whole. Once you get through all 12 Steps, the chapter "Staying the Course" will give you some invaluable tips for staying engaged in your practice, and for getting back on track when you get distracted by changes in your life.

The 12 Steps are not all there is to mindfulness meditation, but they're enough to give you a solid foundation of the practice. Once you've developed some proficiency with your observation skills, you'll be ready for more advanced techniques, such as the Four Establishments of Mindfulness. As you can see, there is practically no limit to how far you can grow with mindfulness meditation.

## How to Use This Book

To get the most out of this book, I recommend that you immediately begin applying the principles you learn in each step as you go along. At the end of each chapter, you'll find a set of exercises to help you put into practice the techniques you just learned. It is easier to put them into practice while they're fresh in your mind, than if you wait until you finish the book. With some of the later steps, you may not be able to implement them right away, but that's OK because this book will serve as a reference for your continued practice.

If you're interested in learning the mindfulness meditation practice even faster, I recommend *The Mindfulness Meditation Workbook*. The exercises in there will go more in-depth to help you develop a deeper understanding of the principles behind the 12 Steps. You can find more information about it on our website.

When you finish reading this book, I suggest that you read it again—this time paying closer attention to the explanations of the techniques. Remember, the whole idea is to learn the proper meditation techniques, and make them the foundation of your practice because it is the proper use of the techniques that will enable you to get the most benefit from your efforts. If you begin to stray from using proper techniques, your progress will suffer.

Next, I recommend that you review the 12 Steps periodically, such as every other month for a while. This will help you avoid developing unwanted habits. As you gain some experience, the explanations will begin to make more sense, and certain nuances of the practice will become apparent.

You can also form a study group, or meditation group, so you can share different perspectives with other practitioners. We've made starting a group very easy with our free group starter kit, which you can download from our website.

I will refer to our website throughout the book because it contains valuable resources and printable copies of various materials you'll need for your practice. I will also address some of the most common issues regarding the practice. Go to http://www.MindfulnessMeditationIn stitute.org and bookmark it, so it is readily available for you.

There is one more important point I would like to make: to get the most from your mindfulness meditation practice, it's important that you apply all 12 Steps, because neglecting any of them will hinder your progress. The good news is that you don't have to do it all at once. You can take it one step at a time, starting with Step 1.

I realize that some techniques might take you out of your comfort zone, but the result will be a happier and more fulfilling life. Your life will change in ways you never imagined. I know that once you get some experience with the Steps, you'll learn to enjoy them as much as I have.

## How to Stay Focused and Committed to Your Practice

I know that sometimes staying committed to a new practice can be a challenge. I want to share with you a couple of tricks I've learned that will help you stay committed to your meditation practice:

1.  Set a goal to learn how to meditate, and write it down. It doesn't have to be a long statement, but be specific. For example, you may set a goal to learn how to meditate in thirty, sixty, or ninety days. Whatever the case, phrase it in your own words and write it down. There is something very powerful about writing down your goals that will help you tremendously in achieving them. Once you learn the basics of the mindfulness meditation practice, set another goal, such as learning one or more of the techniques for enhancing your practice.

2.  Once you've written your initial goal of learning how to meditate, choose two or three people you know and respect, who would most likely support you in your practice. Your meditation group would be great. Share with them the following two things, (1) your goals of learning how to meditate, and (2) how you're learning the practice.

Then periodically mention to them how you're progressing. By openly declaring your commitment, you trigger a powerful mechanism in your mind that helps you follow through on your commitment. You are now accountable to other people, and this makes it harder to go back on your word. In my case, by writing this book I've essentially declared to the world that I practice mindfulness meditation. There's no going back now, which suits me just fine.

## The Courage to Change

One of the greatest obstacles to our spiritual growth is self-deception. It is often difficult to confront the truth of who we are. We all would like to believe that we are kind, loving, and compassionate, and that our intentions are always noble. On the other hand, we sometimes think the worst of ourselves, that we're no-good rotten scoundrels. The truth lies somewhere in between.

If we are going to grow, then we must be willing to face the truth about ourselves. We must be willing to look at ourselves objectively, and let go of our beliefs, no matter how long we've had them. We must have the courage to let go of our old self, if we want our True Nature to shine through. So, are you willing to do what it takes to grow?

~

The Mindfulness Revolution is a movement whose time has come. Every day, more and more people just like you are taking up the practice. Mindfulness meditation is gaining ever wider acceptance, as scientific research confirms the benefits to all areas of our personal lives. The practice is also transforming just about every area of our society, including health care, education, the economy, and even politics.

> If you want to change the world, you must first change yourself.

If you are new to mindfulness meditation, you're about to venture on a journey that will transform your life in ways you never imagined possible. You will experience better health, more stable emotions, and higher self-esteem. Your practice will not only enrich your own life, but also the lives of people around you.

The 12 Steps of the Mindfulness Meditation Practice will give you a solid foundation of the practice as quickly as possible. You will learn how to develop mental discipline, and deep insights into the nature of the human condition. As you implement these techniques, you'll discover for yourself that true inner peace is well within your reach, no matter how restless your mind may be.

Once you begin this spiritual journey, you will no longer be a spectator. You will become a leader in the evolution of human consciousness, and a pioneer in the Mindfulness Revolution. As you realize inner peace, you will naturally want to share the practice with others. The innate wisdom that is within you will be revealed, and will need to express itself through service to mankind. How you serve is entirely up to you. But always remember this: if you want to change the world, you must first change yourself.

## Exercises for Getting Started

I know you're eager to get started. In order to get the most from your practice, it's important to understand the reasons for the specific techniques. However, you can still benefit tremendously by starting the practice right now. Then as you study each Step, you'll begin to understand the practice better. Follow these simple exercises and you'll be off to a good start.

**1. Setting Your Goals.** As described earlier, write down your goals for learning mindfulness meditation. Be specific. For example, set a goal to learn how to meditate in thirty, sixty, or ninety days, and commit to practicing every day; then choose two or three people you know and respect, and who will likely support you in your practice. Tell them about your goals, and how you're learning meditation.

I would also suggest posting your goal statement some place where you'll see it every day. Your computer monitor and mirror are ideal places. If you need help writing it, you can download the goal statement exercise from the Resources page of our website. I have also included it in the appendix.

**2. Sitting Meditation.** Find a quiet time and place where you will not be disturbed for about twenty minutes. Get in a comfortable sitting position, and gently close your eyes. Begin following your breathing. Use the counting technique to help you stay focused. During your meditation, count your breaths one through five silently in your mind. When you get to five, simply start over again.

Keep your attention focused on the air passing through the tip of your nose. It's OK if you get distracted. Simply bring your attention back to your breath, and keep counting. The purpose of this is to help you develop your ability to concentrate.

After a few minutes, stop counting, but continue observing your breath. However, this time instead of counting each one, simply observe the entire breathing process mindfully. Observe it gently without forcing yourself like you did with the concentration meditation. When distracting thoughts arise, gently bring your attention back to your breath.

You can start with 10-15 minutes of total meditation time daily. Then work your way up to thirty minutes or more. Later in the book, I'll explain in more detail the purpose of concentration and mindfulness.

**3.  Writing Meditation.** From the appendix, take the loving-kindness writing meditation exercise and spend about 10-15 minutes each day writing it out by hand. I generally write two verses each day right before my sitting meditation session, but any time of the day will work. This will help you stay focused and committed to your practice. For your convenience, you'll find printable versions of this exercise in the Resources section of our website.

# STEP 1

## Personal Freedom Begins with Understanding Your Suffering

*A journey of a thousand miles begins with a single step.*

~ Lao Tzu

### Chapter Highlights

- The Four Noble Truths and the Nature of Suffering
- The Five Hindrances: The Thieves of Your Spiritual Growth
- How to Overcome the Five Hindrances
- Conclusion
- Exercises

**Step 1**    *"We became aware of the pain and suffering created by unmindful thoughts, speech, and actions."*

M OST OF US SPEND OUR whole lives searching for happiness, and sadly, some of us never find it. I spent a great deal of time and effort searching, but usually ended up unhappy. What I thought would make me happy really didn't; or if I found something that did, the effect was usually short-lived. It wasn't until I had a better understanding of happiness—but more importantly, freedom from suffering—that I was able to achieve long-lasting inner peace.

We have many misconceptions about happiness. We generally think of happiness as feeling good, or satisfied. So we spend our lives chasing things that bring us pleasure, such as material possessions, recognition, achievements, relationships, food, and more. Some people even search for pleasure through drugs and alcohol.

*"Happiness is not something ready made. It comes from your own actions."*

~ DALAI LAMA

While these things do indeed bring us some gratification, the feelings don't last because they are based on sensual pleasure, or emotional satisfaction, which are only temporary. When the pleasant feelings wear off, we need more of the objects of our desires to recreate the same feelings. Sometimes we need a great deal of sensual or emotional gratification just to feel normal. We will never find long-lasting peace until we stop searching for happiness this way.

The practice of mindfulness takes a different approach. Instead of seeking temporary sensual pleasure, we identify and remove the sources of our suffering. We may not fully realize it, but we all have suffering in our lives. Whether it is mild or intense, it all robs us of our inner peace. If we eliminate the sources of our suffering, then the only thing that will remain is long-lasting inner peace.

> By becoming aware of the obstacles to our practice, we can remove them and speed up our transformation.

In Step 1, I will introduce you to some basic principles of the mindfulness meditation practice. We will first discuss the Four Noble Truths, which deal with the nature of suffering. It is important to understand our suffering, if we're going to overcome it. Next, we will discuss the Five Hindrances, which deal with the obstacles to our spiritual growth. By becoming aware of these obstacles, we can remove them and speed up our transformation.

These principles are part of the foundation of the mindfulness meditation practice, so I'll be referring to them throughout the 12 Steps. They are pretty straightforward and easy to understand. Once you understand them, you'll be able to structure your meditation practice for greater effectiveness.

## The Four Noble Truths and the Nature of Suffering

If we want to attain freedom from suffering, we first need to understand what suffering is. In Buddhism, the nature of suffering is summed up in the Four Noble Truths:

1. The existence of suffering
2. The origins of suffering
3. The cessation of suffering
4. The path that leads to the cessation of suffering

### The Existence of Suffering

You probably have a basic understanding of what suffering is, but what may be harder to understand is how deeply it pervades our very existence. Essentially, suffering is ongoing emotional pain. There are varying degrees of suffering, from mild discomfort to outright anguish. It is easy to see our suffering in situations that are obviously painful, such as when a loved one is ill, or when he dies.

Very often, we're not fully aware of our suffering. Now this may sound a bit unusual to some people. We figure that if we feel pain, then we're certainly going to know it. But that isn't always the case. Sometimes our suffering is deep in our subconscious, so it's easier to ignore. Suffering can be like the sound of the refrigerator; you don't realize it's there until it stops. Nevertheless, it is still there and manifesting itself in our life.

> While suffering is part of being human, it doesn't necessarily mean that we're powerless over it.

Some situations cause us pain and suffering without us fully realizing it. Here are some examples:

- How do you feel when you're stuck in traffic, or when someone follows too close behind you?
- How do you feel when you're stressed out, or when you work with people who are difficult to get along with?
- How do you feel when you have an argument with a loved one?
- How about when your political party loses an election?

Any discomfort that arises from these types of situations is suffering, and is keeping us from being at peace.

Many of us believe that our suffering is caused by conditions outside of ourselves, and that we don't have control over it. We figure it's simply part of being human. While suffering is indeed part of being human, it doesn't necessarily mean that we're powerless over it. Just because we haven't been able to do something in the past, doesn't mean we're not capable of doing it. Maybe we just haven't yet learned how.

### The Origins of Suffering

One of the causes of our suffering is our misunderstanding of the way things really are. We often have trouble in our relationships with loved ones because our ignorance causes us to unknowingly say or do harmful things—therefore, compromising our harmony with them.

For example, a loved one may be upset and treat us unkindly. It could be for any number of reasons: a bad day at work, a flat tire, dealing with bad news, or any combination of things. We may not understand the reasons for his behavior, but we often react by taking it personally and treating him unkindly in return, making the situation worse.

Another cause of suffering is clinging, or attachment. We often cling to material things, such as, houses, cars, jobs, and money because we believe these are the sources of our happiness. I've seen people cling to such simple things as a particular seat or parking space. These things may bring us temporary sensual pleasure, but this is not happiness. Being separated from material things can be just as painful as being separated from loved ones. It is still suffering.

We also cling to views. Many of us have strong attachments to political views. We think that if only our political party was in control, then the world would be a much better place. Our views bring us comfort and security because they give us a sense of control and understanding of the world. They are also a part of our identity.

One of the most painful attachments is to an unhealthy relationship. Some people are willing to endure all kinds of abuse just for a few rare moments of intimacy with their partner. They will needlessly sacrifice their dignity and self-respect. In a healthy relationship, all interactions are on a deeper spiritual level. Partners always treat each other with respect, even when they have disagreements.

Some of us are attached to charity work, or some other noble cause. These too can be obstacles to our spiritual growth. It isn't the charity work itself that is the obstacle, but rather our attachment to it. We can still do the work without being attached, and by not being attached to it, we become open to greater opportunities for being of service. When we let go of personal motives, then our charity work will truly be selfless.

Probably the greatest attachment of all is to our ego, that is, our sense of self. Our ego tries everything it can to validate its existence by constantly searching for meaning in our life. It sees the world in terms of me, myself, and I. It keeps us asking the question, "What's in it for me?"

The ego will usually lead us down the wrong path because its main objective is its own survival—and not necessarily peace and serenity. When we begin to awaken our True Nature and see our interconnectedness with other people, we'll see that the ego is actually an illusion of a separate self.

> We cannot be truly selfless until we let go of our self.

As long as we remain attached to our ego, relationships will be difficult. We cannot be truly selfless until we let go of our self. Otherwise, our good deeds will be tainted with personal motives. Letting go of our ego takes mindfulness and courage, but it can be done.

## The Cessation of Suffering

The Third Noble Truth tells us that it is possible to end suffering. I know this from personal experience. As I became stronger spiritually, I was able to let go of my attachments because I no longer needed them. Many of them came in the form of material things and accomplishments that made me feel important. I saw them as a way of finding purpose and meaning to my life.

Once I saw that my life consisted of much more than my material possessions and accomplishments, these things became less important and I was able to let them go. Now, this didn't mean that I gave away all my material possessions. I only let go of my mental and emotional attachments to them. My identity and self-esteem no longer depended on them. That is when much of my suffering began to dissipate.

## The Path that Leads to the Cessation of Suffering

Throughout the ages, many have sought the path to inner peace. Some have discovered that the way to achieve inner peace was by ending our suffering. The Buddha's approach to end suffering was through the

Noble Eightfold Path:

1. Right view
2. Right thinking
3. Right speech
4. Right action
5. Right livelihood
6. Right effort
7. Right mindfulness
8. Right concentration

As you can see, these are common sense principles for conducting ourselves in our daily affairs, but they can be a challenge to actually put into practice. A whole book can be written on the Noble Eightfold Path, so I won't go into a long explanation of each. Instead, I'll show you how to put them into practice through the 12 Steps. By the time you finish this book, you'll have a solid understanding of how to apply them into your daily life, and you'll be well on your way to achieving inner peace and serenity.

## The Five Hindrances: The Thieves of Your Spiritual Growth

Now let's look at some of the obstacles to our spiritual growth. Let me ask you this: have you ever been stuck in traffic and thought to yourself, "If it weren't for all these other cars on the road, I would get to work (or home) much faster"? Well, spiritual development is similar to that. If it weren't for the mental and emotional obstacles, we could develop mindfulness much faster.

There are several common obstacles, and by becoming aware of them, we can minimize their effect on us. In Buddhism, these are called the Five Hindrances:

- **Sensual desire.** This is our desire to please our five senses and emotions.

- **Aversion.** This is a dislike for someone or something. It is the opposite of desire. We naturally try to avoid things that are unpleasant.

- **Lethargy.** This is a mental dullness that arises from boredom, or lack of mental stimulation. It is the result of not being able to enjoy the present moment.

- **Agitation.** This is essentially the opposite of lethargy. It is the over-stimulation of our mind.

- **Doubt.** This is a lack of conviction or trust in our meditation practice.

## Sensual Desire

In order to understand the Five Hindrances better, it might be helpful to understand some of our basic human instincts. Growing up, most of us develop some concept of what happiness is, and how to attain it. In our society, we are encouraged to pursue our dreams, because we're told that they will bring us happiness. These dreams usually consist of a successful career, home-ownership, finding a mate, and settling down. For some people, their dreams may consist of something entirely different. Whatever the case, these achievements bring us some form of emotional gratification, or a pleasing of our senses—that is, they fulfill our desires.

Sensual desire becomes a hindrance because it occupies a tremendous amount of our attention. We spend a great deal of time, money, and effort chasing our desires. The way sensual desire manifests itself during our meditation is through fantasizing. We think about things like food, sex, money, or anything else that brings us gratification.

What's more, we begin to develop a tolerance to the objects of our desires. So when the pleasant feelings wear off, we need even more of these objects to bring us the same level of satisfaction. This is especially true in intimate relationships. The cycle never ends because there is no end to our wants and desires. Some people spend their whole lives chasing material possessions, only to find out that they don't bring them lasting happiness.

This approach to achieving happiness may have served us well in the past. But now that we're on a spiritual path, we want to grow beyond this level. Through the practice of mindfulness, we can achieve an inner peace that is more stable. Our happiness will no longer depend on outside conditions, which we don't have control over, but rather our spiritual condition, which we do have control over.

## Aversion

Aversion is a dislike for something. It can be a dislike of a person, place, event, or memory. It works almost the same way as desire, only in the opposite direction. We try to avoid anything that triggers unpleasant emotions, so we spend a great deal of our time seeking pleasure and avoiding pain.

Aversion can also manifest itself into anger, or ill will. We usually get angry when someone hurts our feelings, or does something we don't like. Anger can be quite seductive and addictive because we sometimes get a rush from it. It's easy to justify our anger because of someone else's injustice. We can also use it to manipulate others into doing what we want.

If we never forgive people for harming us, we'll continue to carry our anger in the form of resentment. In extreme cases, that anger can turn into a deep hatred. Hanging on to anger and resentment will prevent us from growing. As somebody once said, "Holding on to anger is like grasping a hot coal with the intent of throwing it at someone else; you are the one who gets burned."

## Lethargy

Lethargy is a state of mental dullness that arises from boredom. I know from personal experience that sleepiness can be a problem when meditating. The degree of lethargy can vary from simple drowsiness to utter torpor. It's usually the result of doing, or being exposed, to something that doesn't stimulate any of our senses or emotions. Now, there's a difference between lethargy and physical fatigue. Lethargy comes from boredom, and fatigue comes from lack of sleep.

Some of us are addicted to excitement. We need to have something exciting going on all the time. If there isn't, then we get either restless or bored. So we try to create some excitement, and that excitement doesn't necessarily have to be positive. We sometimes even create chaos in our lives to keep the adrenaline going. This is how we become addicted to drama.

## Agitation

Agitation is essentially the opposite of lethargy. It is the over-stimulation of our mind. To avoid getting bored, we do things to occupy our mind, such as watching TV, listening to the radio, or getting involved in many activities. Now, these activities aren't necessarily bad, but we often unconsciously use them to create noise in our mind, so that we keep uncomfortable thoughts from arising.

> The way to stop worrying is to change our understanding of what creates happiness.

We sometimes play the radio or television in the background to keep us company. This stimulates our mind so much that we're not able to sit still. Then we need more noise to drown out the noise that's already there. It's a vicious cycle.

Agitation also manifests itself in the form of worry. We worry about losing the things we think will bring us happiness, such as relationships, money, and material things. We also worry about our health and our mortality. There is never a shortage of things to worry about. The way to stop worrying is to change our understanding of what creates happiness.

## Doubt

The fifth hindrance, doubt, is a lack of conviction and trust. It is the inability to decide on which course of action to follow because we don't know which is best. In meditation, it takes the form of questioning our practice. We start wondering if this meditation stuff really works, or if it's a big waste of time.

Doubt has its roots in fear and ignorance. If we don't understand a situation very well, we become afraid to make the wrong decision. So we begin thinking too much, and become unable to make any decision. This may be more common in the beginning of your practice, but will diminish once you have some experience.

## How to Overcome the Five Hindrances

So how do we overcome the Five Hindrances in our meditation practice? It's actually quite simple. What we're essentially going to do is watch them to death. Of course, this is easier said than done, but not as hard as you might think. Here's how it works: think about a time when you were doing something wrong, for example, driving too fast. Now suppose you drove past a police officer parked on the side of the road, and he watched you as you drove by. What was your first reaction? You stopped speeding, of course. That's a natural reaction.

> Meditation is like any other skill—the more you practice, the better you'll get at it.

When we know someone is watching us do something wrong, we immediately stop. We will deal with the Five Hindrances in the same manner. We're going to stand guard like the police officer on the side of the road, and watch for that speeding motorist when he passes by. That is, we're going to be mindful of the hindrances when they arise, and when they dissipate.

We have to be especially mindful of lethargy, because it can gain momentum very quickly, and before we know it, we're falling asleep.

In the beginning of our practice, we need to learn how to identify the hindrances when they arise by consciously naming them. After some practice, we'll be able to recognize them more easily and just be mindful of their presence.

By practicing this way, we'll remove these obstacles of our meditation, and begin to develop mindfulness much faster. Remember, meditation is like any other skill—the more you practice, the better you'll get at it.

The last thing I would like to say about the hindrances is that we may get upset with ourselves when we lose our concentration or mindfulness during meditation. Don't expect perfection. Maintaining our concentration and mindfulness can be challenging. The good news is that with practice, the hindrances will become less of a problem. In addition, when we observe the hindrances as they arise, we are actually practicing mindfulness. By being aware of them, we are being mindful. So let them come up. Eventually, they will diminish.

## Conclusion

In Step 1, we dispelled some of the misconceptions about happiness. Instead of trying to fulfill our never-ending desires, we're going to find long-lasting peace and serenity through the elimination of our suffering. Then we'll be at peace regardless of what is happening in our life. We take this approach because searching for happiness through sensual desire is a futile effort, as our emotions are fleeting.

*"Happiness for a reason is just another form of misery because the reason can be taken away from us at any time."*

~ Deepak Chopra

In Step 2, you will learn how to develop your skills of observation, so that you're able to see yourself and the world with greater clarity. You will also learn about the sources of spiritual nourishment, the Three Jewels. These will complete the foundation of your mindfulness meditation practice.

As you can see, these principles are pretty straightforward and easy to understand. By reexamining some of the misconceptions about happiness, you've taken a major step toward finding freedom from your suffering. You're now well on your way to taking control of your life and achieving true inner peace.

## Exercises

The following exercises will help you gain a deeper understanding of the nature of your suffering, and its sources. Write down your answers in a notebook.

**1. Identifying Suffering.** Give some examples of suffering in your life. Begin with obviously painful situations. Then give examples of suffering that may not be so obvious, such as mild anxiety, annoyances, cravings for certain things (e.g. food, pleasure, money, and other material things). How does it feel when you don't get what you want?

**2. Identifying Attachments.** Identify things in your life to which you are attached emotionally. These may be material possessions, people, or views. Why are they so important? Are your identity and self-esteem associated with these things? What would happen if you let go of them?

**3. Understanding the Five Hindrances.** Write down in your own words the definition of each of the Five Hindrances. Then give some examples of how they manifest themselves in your life.

# STEP 2

## Concentration and Mindfulness: The Tools for Expanding Your Awareness

*Knowing yourself is the beginning of all wisdom.*

~ ARISTOTLE

### Chapter Highlights

- Concentration: The Anchor of the Peaceful Mind
- Mindfulness: Your Key to Enlightenment
- The Three Jewels: Your Sources of Spiritual Nourishment
- Conclusion
- Exercises

**Step 2**   *"We learned how to develop our primary tools of observation: concentration and mindfulness."*

WHEN I WAS A KID, I once asked my mom for permission to do something all my friends were doing, which she thought was ridiculous. She responded by asking me, "If all your friends were to jump off a bridge, would you follow them?" It made me so angry because I couldn't argue with her, yet I still felt driven to follow my friends.

We all have our own views about relationships and the world, which determine our actions. Our views are shaped by our experiences, upbringing, family traditions, role models, and peers. Eventually, these views make up our philosophy about life, and the world in general.

> *"Awareness is the greatest agent for change."*
>
> ~ ECKHART TOLLE

The problem with this approach to shaping our views is that the views handed down to us were not entirely accurate. We often accept views without fully examining them, or maybe we'll add our reasoning afterward so we can justify our conclusions. This is not sound reasoning. What we're essentially doing is putting the cart before the horse.

We often accept views, or opinions, based on the way they make us feel, rather than unbiased observation and reasoning. However, our emotions are not good indicators of the truth because they are rooted in our ego, which will do anything to justify its relevance to our existence. We accept other people's views because they give us a sense of identity and belonging. They may also give us a sense of security.

We will not find freedom from our suffering until we see the world as it truly is. We need to learn to observe it without our perceptions being influenced by our emotions, or preconceived ideas. Once we're able to see the true nature of reality, we'll see that the ego is an illusion that keeps us separate from the rest of humanity. Then painful emotions will subside, and we'll realize that the world is not the cold and lonely place we once thought it was.

In Step 2, we'll take a close look at the principles of concentration and mindfulness. These are our primary tools of observation. It's important to develop some proficiency with them, so that we can see the true nature of our existence. I'll show you how to put them into practice later in the Steps.

The concentration and mindfulness that we're seeking are at a much deeper level than what we're familiar with. By developing concentration, we'll be better able to give our attention to the objects of our observation. By developing mindfulness, we'll be better able to look deeper into all phenomena and see the true nature of reality—and this is the key to liberation.

I will also introduce you to the Three Jewels: the Buddha, the Dharma, and the Sangha. These are the sources of spiritual nourishment we need to grow, and to provide us with the light to help us see reality with greater clarity. I will show you how to put these into practice throughout the 12 Steps.

> Both concentration and mindfulness work together to help us look deeply into the true nature of reality.

Through the mindfulness meditation practice, you will reach a level of mental discipline that few people attain. It takes some diligence and commitment, but your reward will be a much greater insight into the nature of the human condition, and you'll be surprised at what you'll see. So buckle your seat belt because you're about to venture on a fascinating journey, and discover the full potential of the human mind.

## Concentration: The Anchor of the Peaceful Mind

Concentration is the ability to focus our attention on one subject or object. We do this by forcing ourselves to pay attention. Mindfulness, on the other hand, is a more delicate activity. It is an awareness of what is happening in the present moment. Both concentration and mindfulness work together to help us look deeply into the true nature of reality.

Our objective is to look deeply at phenomena to see things that are not readily apparent to the average person. This requires the ability to keep our attention fixed on an object without being distracted by the Five Hindrances (sensual desire, aversion, lethargy, agitation, and doubt). In order for concentration to be effective for our purposes, it must contain three important qualities: (1) it must be wholesome, (2) it must be one-pointed, and (3) it must function with mindfulness.

Concentration is wholesome when it is free of any of the Five Hindrances. For example, if we're able to concentrate deeply on a task with the main objective to seek revenge, then it is unwholesome because it is tainted with aversion. This will not lead to liberation because our motives are rooted in our ego. This form of concentration will keep us attached to our ego, and we'll be unable to see our interconnectedness with the rest of humanity.

Sometimes, an activity can be either wholesome or unwholesome, depending on our motives behind it. If we concentrate on a task with the purpose of amassing great material wealth for ourselves, then it is unwholesome because our motives would be rooted in greed, which is a form of sensual desire. On the other hand, the same activity with the purpose of helping others who are less fortunate would be considered wholesome.

When we are meditating, some of our distractions manifest themselves into negative emotions. If we dwell on them, then our concentration will be unwholesome. If we want to see the roots of our suffering, our concentration must be wholesome. There is another reason for developing wholesome concentration; it will also help us transform our thoughts, speech, and actions throughout our daily lives.

One-pointedness refers to concentration without being distracted by the Five Hindrances. This may be more of a challenge to accomplish. It takes practice to achieve, but once we do, our concentration will be more powerful and we'll be able to see much deeper into the subject of our meditation.

For concentration to be useful, we must be able to use it in conjunction with mindfulness, because it is with mindfulness that we select the object of our meditation, and become aware of when our mind has gone astray.

## Mindfulness: Your Key to Enlightenment

In order to develop deep concentration, it's important to have an environment that is free from distractions, because they can trigger the Hindrances and interrupt our concentration. That is why Buddhist monks go to great lengths to create such an environment. This is not necessary with mindfulness, because with mindfulness we simply notice whatever is happening.

Mindfulness is neither wholesome nor unwholesome. Our attention is free to move from one object to another. This is the main difference between concentration and mindfulness. With concentration, we force our mind to pay attention to one object, and with mindfulness we gently observe it.

Mindfulness is a powerful tool of observation. However, it cannot be developed by force like we do with concentration. In fact, trying to force ourselves to be mindful is counterproductive, because the purpose of mindfulness is to simply observe without attachment. Now, this doesn't mean that mindfulness develops all by itself. On the contrary, it requires effort and energy. We develop mindfulness by consciously paying attention to what is happening in the present moment. When our mind wanders off during meditation, with mindfulness we can gently bring it back.

Mindfulness is ego-less and non-discriminating. Since its function is to simply notice what is actually happening, it does so regardless of what it finds. It helps us examine our true nature and the motives behind our behavior, thinking, and emotions. It is mindfulness that will help us develop wisdom.

I'm sure you've already experienced mindfulness before. For example, when we find a beautiful flower, we usually just observe and enjoy its beauty in the present moment, without judgment or attachment. Sometimes, certain situations compel us to be in the present moment, like when we go on vacation to an unfamiliar place. We don't know exactly what to expect, and the unfamiliarity of our surroundings draws our attention to the events taking place in the present moment. Have you noticed how it makes you feel? This is one way vacations help us relax.

> *"When you touch one thing with deep awareness, you touch everything."*
> ~ THICH NHAT HANH

There is one challenge to developing mindfulness through our meditation practice; some of the things we become aware of may not be so pleasant. Practicing mindfulness is like casting a wide net; you'll catch all kinds of things, even some you never intended. We will notice some things about ourselves that we may not like very much, or bring up painful memories, but don't worry. Through the practice, you'll learn how to look at yourself objectively and develop the inner strength to accept what you see, and this will enable you to overcome painful memories once and for all. I'll show you exactly how to do this in Step 11.

It is important to have a balanced development of both concentration and mindfulness, because each supports the development of the other. Otherwise, we won't be able to see the roots of our suffering. Mindfulness enables us select wholesome objects of meditation, and concentration enables us to look deeply into their nature.

If we only develop concentration, then we become so tranquilized that our practice becomes of little benefit to anyone. On the other hand, if we develop mindfulness without concentration, then our awareness will be scattered and superficial, and this certainly will not lead to liberation.

In the beginning of a meditation practice, there may be a tendency to focus too much on mindfulness alone, because it is easier to just let our mind wander and observe the constant stream of thoughts. Some forms of meditation emphasize this type of practice. Don't fall into this trap. Make sure you practice concentration regularly. In fact, I recommend that in the beginning you place more emphasis on concentration than on mindfulness. Once you've developed some measure of concentration and your mind is no longer racing, then you can work more on mindfulness.

> What you're aiming for is steady progress, not perfection.

During those times when your mind is restless, emphasize concentration. When your mind is getting lethargic, emphasize mindfulness. Remember that it takes time to develop these skills, but you certainly will if you are diligent. One way to make good progress is by attending a retreat where the environment is conducive to their development, so you can dedicate all your attention to the practice for a few days. We'll talk more about that soon.

One important thing to remember; what you're aiming for is steady progress, not perfection. In the beginning, it may be a challenge to stop the constant stream of distracting thoughts. That is normal. If you have just a few brief moments of good concentration or mindfulness, consider it a success. As you continue practicing, your concentration will become deeper, and it will last longer. This is how we progress. So, celebrate your successes!

## The Three Jewels: Your Sources of Spiritual Nourishment

There is one more important quality about mindfulness that we have not yet discussed. Mindfulness is more than simply awareness. It is a form of energy, the energy of consciousness. Each spiritual tradition has a different name for it. The Buddhists call it the energy of mindfulness, because it shines the light on reality. It is the spiritual nourishment we need to awaken our higher consciousness.

Think about a time in your life when you felt some form of spiritual connection. It may have been when you were especially close to someone, or you may have had a profound spiritual experience. At the time, you probably gained some clarity in your life, felt more peaceful and secure, and felt a great sense of love. You may even have sensed a connection with a power much greater than yourself. That is the energy of mindfulness that we're trying to cultivate through our mediation practice.

> Mindfulness energy is the spiritual nourishment we need to awaken our higher consciousness.

The major religions are similar in their approach to raising your spiritual energy. There are three main sources. In Buddhism, they're called the Three Jewels:

- **The Buddha.** Our own Buddha Nature, higher consciousness, True Nature, or spirit
- **The Dharma.** The spiritual principles that govern our existence
- **The Sangha.** The spiritual community that supports our practice

These sources of spiritual nourishment are vital to our development of mindfulness, and can significantly speed up our spiritual evolution. By dwelling in them, we can transform our unwholesome thoughts and actions. When you put them into practice, I think you'll find that they will greatly enhance your meditation. In short, the Three Jewels will help you grow much faster.

## Your Buddha Nature

There are different interpretations of the Buddha when referring to the Three Jewels. Some interpret it as the historical Buddha who lived 2,500 years ago, and others interpret it as the highest ideal of our being—the essence of who we really are. For our purposes, we're going to use the latter interpretation. While we owe a great debt of gratitude to the historical Buddha, I think it would be more practical for us to seek and dwell in our own Buddha Nature. We will sometimes refer to it as our True Nature.

Our Buddha Nature is actually the most powerful of all the Three Jewels, but it is also the most difficult to connect with. Some of us stumble into it by accident. You may have had a profound spiritual experience where you were in touch with a higher level of consciousness. If you're fortunate to have had such an experience, you've gotten a glimpse of the Buddha within you.

Keep in mind that you don't need to have such a profound experience to get in touch with your Buddha Nature. You can also connect with it through diligent practice of mindfulness meditation. You can make steady progress this way.

## The Dharma

The Dharma is defined as the teachings of the Buddha. It is essentially the whole set of spiritual principles that will help us achieve enlightenment. Each religion's founder left us with a set of universal spiritual principles. The interpretations are slightly different among the major religions, and even within Buddhism, because only a fully awakened person truly understands them. Furthermore, the cultures that adopted the spiritual practices have influenced their interpretations, but they're essentially the same.

Buddhism has many spiritual principles. So far, we've covered the Four Noble Truths, the Five Hindrances, and the Three Jewels. There are many more such as the Noble Eightfold Path, Seven Factors of Awakening, and the Four Establishments of Mindfulness. But don't worry about all those now. If you concentrate on the ones we've covered, you'll make a great deal of progress. In time, all the others will become much easier to understand, and in many cases, they will become obvious as you develop mindfulness.

By dwelling in the Dharma, we're basically living our lives according to universal principles, so we can enhance our spiritual development. It is like swimming with the current, instead of against it. What we're essentially doing is speeding up our spiritual evolution. This will lead to harmony within ourselves, and with the world around us.

## The Sangha

The Sangha (or meditation group) is the spiritual community that supports our practice. I know some of you prefer to practice alone. While this is an important aspect of your practice, you can make much faster progress by also meditating with others. Under the right circumstances, meditating with others can be very powerful.

> A sangha is an essential source of mindfulness energy.

A synergy takes place when we meditate with others. When we open our heart to others, we connect with their Buddha Nature and the energy of mindfulness flows freely, which is much harder to do when meditating alone. To whom do we open our heart when we're alone? This is why it's so important to practice regularly with a meditation group, in addition to practicing alone. Both serve an important purpose.

When you join a sangha, you will become part of a community where you can share your experiences and challenges. You will meet a group of like-minded people that will support you by helping you stay engaged in your practice. A sangha is an essential source of mindfulness energy.

Don't worry if there aren't any sanghas near you that practice mindfulness meditation because starting a group is amazingly simple. All it takes is two people who enjoy meditation, and you can start by meeting at your house. If you spread the word, soon your sangha will be thriving. If you need help getting started, you can download the free group starter kit from our website.

In Steps 7 and 12, I'll show you exactly how to start your own sangha. I'll share with you some valuable tips, and you'll see just how simple it really is, even if you're a novice in the practice. What makes it so easy is that you'll have other people who are just as enthusiastic as yourself to help you.

Another form of sangha is the mindfulness meditation retreat. Without a doubt, this is the most effective because everyone who attends is completely focused on his meditation practice for several days. The mindfulness energy that is harnessed at a retreat is many times greater than that of a weekly meeting, or practicing by ourselves. You can make months, if not years, worth of progress in just a matter of days. You can literally feel the energy and see the transformation taking place right before your eyes.

For the serious meditator, the mindfulness meditation retreat is the ultimate source of mindfulness energy. It is a powerful and effective way of speeding up your spiritual development, and unbeatable for dramatically building your motivation and enthusiasm. Just about everyone I've seen attend a retreat, has been able to stay committed to his meditation practice. It is an indispensable tool for anyone serious about meditation. It will take your spirituality to a much higher level, and quickly.

The Three Jewels complement each other very well. They are the optimal combination of sources for harnessing the energy of mindfulness necessary for nourishing our spiritual evolution. By dwelling in the Three Jewels, you'll be able to maximize the impact of your efforts. The result will be a much shorter path to inner peace.

## Conclusion

In Step 2, we covered more of the principles necessary for an effective meditation practice. Concentration and mindfulness are your main tools of observation, and the Three Jewels provide you with the spiritual nourishment you need to grow. These principles, along with those you learned in Step 1, make up the foundation of the mindfulness meditation practice, and I'll refer to them throughout the book.

These principles enable you to see the true nature of your pain and suffering, so you can eliminate their sources. I'll show you how to apply them as we progress through the 12 Steps. Once you put them into practice, they will become skills, and the more proficient you become with them, the faster you will grow.

As you develop these skills, you'll be able to resist the temptation to blindly accept other people's views and opinions. In other words, you won't have to follow your friends off the bridge. You'll be able to see for yourself the true nature of your existence. This is your path to inner peace.

## Exercises

The following exercises will help you develop an understanding of the basic concepts we covered in Step 2. The better you understand them, the faster you will grow when you put them into practice.

**1. Concentration and Mindfulness.** Review the explanations of concentration and mindfulness. Then write down in your own words the definition of each. What is the difference between the two?

**2. The Three Jewels.** Review the explanation of the Three Jewels. Then write down in your own words the definition of each. Explain why they're so important to your spiritual development.

# STEP 3

## How to Control Your Racing Mind for Peace and Serenity

*To enjoy good health, to bring true happiness to one's family, to bring peace to all, one must first discipline and control one's own mind.*

~ The Teachings of Buddha

### Chapter Highlights

- How the Mind Works
- Why Can't I Sit Still?
- How to Slow Down Your Mind
- Conclusion
- Exercises

**Step 3**    *"We sought to eliminate the things that agitate our mind, and prevent us from achieving inner peace and serenity."*

THERE IS AN OLD BUDDHIST story about a man riding a horse, which is used to illustrate what a racing mind does to us. One day, the man was riding his horse quickly down the road and with great determination. A bystander shouted to him, "Where are you going?" The man on the horse replied, "I don't know. Ask the horse!" Our racing mind does the same thing to us: it takes us for a ride, and we don't know where it's going.

A racing mind is a serious problem for some of us. Our lives are filled with commitments to our jobs, families, and friends. Most of these commitments are necessary, including social activities. We all want to be productive and feel like there is a place for us in the world, so we take on as many commitments as possible—sometimes too many.

The problem with taking on too many commitments is that they over-stimulate our mind, and rob us of our peace and serenity. We don't give our mind a chance to settle down and process all the information it has received through our senses, and we certainly don't give it a chance to heal from the wounds of our past. Our thoughts gain so much momentum that it becomes almost impossible to sit still and meditate. Furthermore, we start becoming less productive because we're not able to focus and be mindful of the consequences of our actions.

> Having a calm mind is not a matter of who you are, but rather what you do.

Some people have the misconception that they need to calm their mind before they start meditating. They often think that they're just the type of person who can't sit still. Having a calm mind is not a matter of who you are, but rather what you do. This is good news for you because it gives you control over your peace and serenity.

In this step, we're going to learn how the mind processes information, so we can identify the sources of our mental agitation, and then I'll show you how to minimize them. I will also show you how to keep your mind from racing by implementing two useful tools: mindful breathing and mindful walking. I think you'll be amazed at how effective they are at calming your mind, thus making your meditation sessions much more productive. I've seen people with ADD and ADHD calm their mind after just one session. You'll see just how easy it is to quiet a racing mind.

## How the Mind Works

It would be helpful to understand some basic thought processing in order to see why our mind gets so agitated. The primary mechanism by which we perceive the world is through our five senses: sight, sound, taste, touch, and smell. These are our receptors. They are connected to our brain and send us raw information about what is taking place around us at any given moment. Each time our senses are stimulated, our brain reacts by interpreting the signals it receives and tries to determine the proper response. In other words, each stimulus triggers a thought, either conscious or unconscious.

For many stimuli, we already have prepared responses that we've learned from experience. These are called conditioned responses. For example, when we were children, we didn't know that touching a hot stove could harm us, even though our parents warned us of the danger. It wasn't until we burned ourselves that we learned the proper response; not to touch a hot stove. From that point forward, we didn't have to think about it; we just kept our hands away from the hot stove. Our response became automatic, or conditioned.

Other situations are more complex. They involve the stimulation of multiple senses and previous experiences, and therefore, take more mental processing to interpret. Over time, our reactions to these situations also become automatic because they save us the time and energy necessary to re-examine familiar situations.

The drawback with conditioned responses is that they may not always be the best responses, because we're usually forced to make decisions without having complete information. The mindfulness meditation practice will improve our ability to see the world on a deeper level, so we'll gain the insight necessary to make better decisions. The main point for now is that any stimulation of our senses triggers thought processes, and too much can lead to mental agitation.

## Why Can't I Sit Still?

If your mind is always racing, then you're probably overwhelmed with activities, which are over-stimulating your mind. Your commitments take up every minute of your day; from the time you wake up, until the time you go to bed. Your mind never gets a rest, not even when you sleep. You may have a fast-paced demanding job, and spend many hours multitasking. And when you get home, you're confronted with family issues, or other commitments that take up your spare time. Then to get some relief, you might get involved in a hobby or another activity to divert your attention from the constant stream of thoughts, but this only makes things worse.

When people ask me how to stop their mind from racing, I tell them to start by taking their foot off the accelerator. Most of us are unaware that our daily activities are the primary sources of our mental agitation. Once we become aware of these sources, we can do something about them. There are four main sources of agitation: (1) too many commitments, (2) background noise, (3) painful memories, and (4) worrying. Let's take a closer look at each.

### Too Many Commitments

Most of us want to be productive, and there's nothing wrong with that. The problem arises when we take on too many commitments without being fully aware of how these activities affect our mind. Many of us have families, so we have long-term commitments to providing for them.

> If our mind is always agitated, then we're unable to be fully present when we're with our loved ones.

Some of us had to endure extreme hardships when we were growing up, and we certainly don't want our children to experience that. So we work hard to give our children all the comforts of life. However, if we don't have a balance between our commitments to our family and personal time, our mind becomes extremely agitated.

If our mind is always agitated, then we're unable to be fully present when we're with our loved ones. Our attention is focused on events happening elsewhere. They may have all the material comforts in life, but they don't have what is most important to them—our presence. We become strangers living in the same house.

Many of us are uncomfortable with idle time, because we unconsciously think that we're not being productive, or that we're not engaged in something meaningful, and this has significant implications regarding our self-esteem. At the root of this discomfort is the ego because it constantly seeks validation by looking for meaning.

In an age of fast-paced careers and multitasking, we have difficulty taking time to relax and rejuvenate ourselves. To deal with this problem, it would be helpful to mindfully examine our commitments. We can do this by asking ourselves some tough questions:

- Do I have any personal time, or is it all filled with commitments to others?

- Is making so much money really contributing to my family's happiness?

- Are my extracurricular activities truly helping me relax, or are they simply drowning out the noise in my head?

I would suggest making a list of all your activities and commitments, including meditation. Remember that your spiritual development is important to your family's happiness, because it will enable you to truly be available to them, both mentally and emotionally. Then prioritize your commitments according to how much they contribute to your and your family's happiness, and give up the least important ones to make time for your personal needs. With many of our commitments, we have no choice in the short-run. We can't quit our job, or abandon our family.

Once you've developed some measure of mindfulness through your meditation practice, you can begin thinking more long-term and restructure your life in order to take your spirituality to a higher level. That is, you can examine your job (or career) and determine whether it is indeed contributing to your family's well-being.

Over the course of my spiritual journey, I've gradually restructured my life so that it's more conducive to my development. I grew up in Miami, where it was crowded and life was fast-paced. In time, I began to realize that a quiet environment would enhance my spiritual growth, so I moved to the outskirts of the city as far as I could. It was much quieter, but there was still a pretty good amount of noise.

At the time, I had a business on the Internet and didn't have to commute to work. I soon realized that an even quieter environment would further enhance my development. That's when I decided to move to the mountains of Western North Carolina. Now, that didn't mean that I wanted to be isolated from society. Quite the contrary; I wanted to enhance my spiritual growth so that I could become a more effective messenger.

## Background Noise

Background noise is another thing that agitates our mind, and much of it is unnecessary. Often when we're driving home after a busy day at work, we'll turn on the radio in our car to help us unwind, all the while, still thinking about work or things we need to do at home, such as checking on the kids or making dinner.

When we get home, then we might turn on the television while we settle in, not really paying attention to what's on. We usually do this unconsciously to drown out the constant chatter in our mind. What we may not realize is that this background noise is agitating our mind even more, and when it becomes unbearable, we might pour ourselves a drink to help us relax.

Some people play the radio or television while they work, thinking this will help them concentrate. The reason this seems to help is that the extra noise prevents uncomfortable thoughts from rising to our conscious mind, but the background noise only creates more agitation.

Sometimes, we'll play the radio or television while we're doing chores. We often have an aversion to silence because uncomfortable thoughts tend to rise to the surface. They can be either painful memories, or thoughts of situations that are causing us stress.

There is nothing inherently wrong with listening to the radio or watching television. When we engage in them mindfully, they can indeed help us relax. I certainly enjoy watching television and listening to music. The problem arises when we use them as background noise. Remember that any stimulus to our senses triggers thought processes, and if we're trying to cultivate a quiet mind, then they're certainly not helping. What I would suggest is not playing the radio or television (or any other entertainment device) when you're doing something else, and focus your attention on the task at hand. This will help you stay in the present moment, and develop concentration and mindfulness.

At the other extreme, I've seen people throw away their radio and television, but this is also not conducive to mindfulness. Keep in mind that these are simply mediums that we use to connect with the rest of the world, and it's difficult to be fully mindful if we're out of touch. The whole idea is to use these tools mindfully, and not to agitate our mind. I think you'll be surprised at how much calmer you will become when you stop using entertainment devices as background noise.

## Painful Memories

We all have memories of loss and injustices that caused us pain and suffering. Unless we've dealt with them, we have an undercurrent of thoughts and emotions that is constantly agitating our mind. Our tendency is to avoid thinking about painful memories, so that we don't re-live the pain and suffering. We often do this by creating some form of noise or distraction, or by putting something into our body to dull our mind, such as alcohol or other substances.

Another way we often keep painful memories at bay is to engage in activities that bring us sensual pleasure, such as food, sex, or even work. We usually do this if we haven't yet learned constructive ways of dealing with adversity or stress. What we're essentially doing is trying to replace negative emotions with positive ones. However, this only covers up the pain temporarily. It doesn't allow the wounds to heal.

> Once the wounds from your past have healed, they will never cause you pain and suffering again.

If you've experienced mental or emotional trauma, then I suggest getting professional help, in addition to your meditation practice. In doing so, I would caution you about using prescription medications, as they just cover up the symptoms. They don't deal with the underlying problem. Of course, always follow the directions of your doctor, but keep in mind that you will only overcome your problems by confronting them.

Most of us have unresolved issues with other people, especially loved ones, and sometimes even with ourselves. If they're not severe enough to require professional help, then your mindfulness meditation practice should suffice in dealing with them. The truth is, they'll take some time and effort to overcome, but once the wounds from your past have healed, they will never cause you pain and suffering again. The good news is that it'll be much easier and less painful than you think, because your meditation practice will give you the inner strength to overcome almost any adversity.

Keep in mind that if you don't deal with the wounds from your past, you'll miss out on the peace and serenity that lie on the other side. In Step 11, I'll show you how to use your meditation practice to heal these wounds. For now, just be aware that they're sources of agitation that will hinder your progress, and stay focused on the basics of the practice.

### Worrying: The Ego's Greatest Ally

Unless we're highly evolved, most of us worry at some time or another. We generally worry about not having our wants and needs met. Some of our biggest worries are about money and financial security. No matter what we worry about, it is all counterproductive and slows our progress.

I should point out that there's a difference between concern and worry. With concern, we acknowledge an issue's importance and our need to address it. On the other hand, worry is a fearful dwelling on the outcome. For example, we may worry about our children having enough to eat, or we can take the necessary actions to get the food they need.

Worry is rooted in the ego because our ego is constantly dwelling on wants and desires. Furthermore, if we're not yet able to see ourselves beyond this physical form, we'll worry about our mortality and of being alone in this world. As you develop mindfulness, you will see that you're more than a physical form, and you're not alone. When this happens, the ego will begin to disappear, and so will worry. In addition, by being mindful of worry immediately as it arises, you can prevent it from gaining momentum, which makes it much easier to deal with.

While worry has its roots in the ego, it gets its fuel from unrealistic thinking. We often think about the worst thing that could happen if we don't get what we want or need. We spend a lot of time and energy creating scenarios in our mind about how bad it will get, and most of them are unrealistic. And even if they are realistic, worrying isn't going to help.

We often worry when we have too much free time on our hands. When we're busy, we don't have time to worry because our mind is occupied with more productive things. When I was early in my spiritual journey, I worried all the time. A friend of mine gave me a clever and simple solution: get involved helping people who are less fortunate than me. I took his suggestion, and it worked. Not only did it keep my mind occupied, but it also helped me get out of myself and put things into perspective. Suddenly, my problems weren't so bad.

Today, I volunteer at the local homeless shelter several times a week, so I never have to worry about my personal problems, and I get a tremendous amount of joy and fulfillment out of it.

## How to Slow Down Your Mind

We usually start our day relaxed and refreshed from a good night's rest. As we engage in our daily activities, we begin thinking about all the things we need to do. When we get to work, we usually have to deal with a variety of issues. The demands on our mind become greater as the day progresses. After a few hours, our mind gains so much momentum that we can't stop the constant stream of thoughts, even after our workday is over.

This happens because we're on the go all day long, often with little or no breaks. How do we expect our mind to slow down if we never take our foot off the accelerator? Fortunately, there are a couple of simple remedies. One is mindful breathing, and the other is mindful walking. Both can dramatically lower the unnecessary chatter in our mind and improve our ability to develop concentration and mindfulness.

### *The Calming Power of Mindful Breathing*

Practicing mindful breathing is very easy and doesn't take long, and it will interrupt the acceleration of your mind. This will enable you to think with greater clarity, since you'll have less mental agitation. All you have to do is stop occasionally and take three to five mindful breaths. You don't have to strain to concentrate on your breathing, but rather just pay attention to it.

Mindful breathing also has other benefits. It reminds us of what we're trying to accomplish through our practice, and it brings us back to the present moment, which is where reality is always taking place. Try it and you'll see the difference it makes. Later in the Steps, I'll show you how to use your breathing as the object of your meditation. For now, we're going to use it to prevent our mind from racing out of control.

### Mindful Walking: Slow Down the Body, and the Mind Will Follow

Practicing mindful walking is also very easy. Most of us do a great deal of walking through our daily activities: at home, work, school, or when tending to our family's needs. These are all great opportunities to practice mindfulness, instead of allowing ourselves to get lost in our thoughts, many of which are worry or simply rehashing the same thoughts repeatedly.

> *"The mind can go in a thousand directions, but on this beautiful path, I walk in peace."*
>
> ~ THICH NHAT HANH

When doing mindful walking, we generally walk more slowly than usual. Make your walking a smooth and continuous movement, while being mindful of each step. This can have a tremendous calming effect because it forces your mind to slow down right along with the rest of your body.

To practice mindful walking, simply pay close attention to your footsteps. With each step, notice the sensation in your feet, the contraction of the muscles in your legs, and the sensation of your clothes against your skin. Not only will this calm your mind, but it will also help you return to the present moment.

One of the best opportunities to practice mindful walking is to and from our vehicle. This is usually a time when we let our mind drift, or we get on our cell phone. Instead, why not use that time to practice mindful walking? You can even do a walking meditation session for a few minutes in a park, or any other suitable quiet place.

## Conclusion

As you've just learned, it's not difficult to slow a racing mind. We do this by becoming aware of the sources of mental agitation, and then taking measures to eliminate them. The four main sources are: too many commitments, background noise, painful memories, and worrying.

You also learned that you have a couple of useful tools for calming your mind further: mindful breathing and mindful walking. When you incorporate them into your daily routine, you'll begin taking control of your mind by improving your ability to concentrate and staying in the present moment.

When you apply these tools, it will become easier to sit and meditate for longer periods of time, and your sessions will become much more productive. Your life

> *"If a man can control his mind he can find the way to Enlightenment, and all wisdom and virtue will naturally come to him."*
>
> ~ THE TEACHINGS OF BUDDHA

will also become more enjoyable because you will stop the mental agitation that is robbing you of your peace and serenity. With a peaceful mind, you will no longer be at the mercy of an undisciplined mind and unpredictable emotions.

In the next step, you're going to learn how to structure your meditation session. We will discuss when, where, and how long to meditate. We will also discuss sitting position. These are individual choices that we each must make. However, I will provide you with guidelines for structuring a meditation session that is most suitable for your needs, and lifestyle.

## Exercises

Exercises 1-4 will help you identify the sources of mental agitation in your life, so you can make changes wherever possible. Exercises 5-7 will help keep your thoughts from gaining too much momentum as you go about your daily activities. I think you'll find that they'll make your meditation much easier, and more productive.

### Identify the Sources of Your Mental Agitation

**1. Commitments.** Make a list of all your commitments and regular activities. Then put them in order of priority. If you don't have any quiet time for yourself, consider giving up the ones with low priority. Keep in mind that you want a balance between commitments to others and to your personal development.

**2. Background noise.** Make a list of all the sources of background noise in your environment (obvious ones and not-so-obvious ones), such as traffic, neighbors, animals, and machinery. Eliminate the ones you can. Then describe what your ideal environment would be like, and think about whether it is within the realm of possibilities.

**3. Painful memories.** At this point, it's not necessary to list your painful memories. As you progress in the Steps, some will come up as you become strong enough to deal with them. For now, just be aware that you will overcome them when you're ready.

**4. Worrying.** If you worry a lot, then I suggest you get involved helping people who are less fortunate than you. The local homeless shelter is always a good place to volunteer, but there are also many other wonderful opportunities. The people you work with are always very grateful for your help. You will gain a tremendous amount of enjoyment and satisfaction from helping them.

### Calming Your Mind

**5. Mindful breathing.** Start by taking two or three short breaks throughout your day to breathe mindfully. Five mindful breaths take only about twenty seconds, so nobody will even know that you're taking a break. A great time to do this is during tense situations. If you like, you can include more such breaks.

**6. Mindful walking.** A great way to start a routine is to designate a particular path that you walk every day as a mindful walking area, such as from your front door to your car, or any other path you walk regularly. Each time you walk that path, remember to walk mindfully. Then you can gradually include other occasions, such as when you need to walk to different places during work.

**7. Walking Meditation.** If you're able, find a quiet place where you can walk for a few minutes, such as a park or trail. Spend about twenty to thirty minutes walking slowly and mindfully. This is almost as effective as sitting meditation for slowing down your mind, and quite enjoyable. I recommend doing this at least once a week.

# STEP 4
## Design Your Meditation Session to Fit Your Lifestyle

*There are only two mistakes one can make along the road to truth; not going all the way, and not starting.*

~ UNKNOWN

### Chapter Highlights

- Finding Your Best Time to Meditate
- Finding a Place Free of Distractions
- Choosing a Sitting Position
- How Long Should I Meditate?
- Conclusion
- Exercises

**Step 4**  *"We learned how to structure our meditation session for maximum effectiveness, and to fit our lifestyle."*

WHEN I FIRST BEGAN MEDITATING, I had heard so many wonderful things about the practice, but I was never told exactly how to do it. I basically just sat quietly for a few minutes, hoping I was doing something right. It helped some, but I never realized how much I was missing until I began applying the mindfulness meditation techniques. It was an eye-opening experience.

We all want results from our meditation practice. We want to see that our time and efforts are paying off. Many people have the misconception that it takes a long time to see results from meditation. It is not that way with mindfulness meditation.

The problem that many beginners, and some experienced meditators, have is that they haven't learned the mechanics of a good meditation practice. They usually do the same thing I did—sit still for a while, and hope for the best. They don't know how to structure their meditation for maximum

> *"The main business is not to see what lies dimly at a distance but to do what lies clearly at hand."*
>
> ~ THOMAS CARLYLE

effectiveness. And if they don't see much result from their practice, they'll soon quit and find a more productive way to spend their valuable time.

As a serious meditator, you understand the importance of paying attention to details. Many factors will affect your development. Some will enhance it, and others will hinder it.

In Step 4, I will show you how to structure your meditation session to help you achieve maximum results, and to fit your personal lifestyle. A well structured meditation session will go a long way toward helping you develop your observation skills, concentration and mindfulness. We'll talk about the time, place, sitting position, and duration of your meditation session. Once you apply the techniques that we'll cover, you'll see results from each session, which is the way it should be.

## Finding Your Best Time to Meditate

The first thing you want to do is establish a formal practice schedule. This is something you will need to determine for yourself. Each of us functions better at different times of the day, some in the mornings, and others in the evenings. Whatever the case, choose a time when you're alert. Mindfulness meditation is not deep relaxation. We're trying to cultivate mental alertness, and not sleep.

> Finding the time to meditate may just be a matter of good time management.

Some people meditate immediately upon waking up. Unless you're a trained firefighter, and can be fully alert as soon as you open your eyes, I recommend not meditating at that time. It takes most of us a little while, and sometimes a cup of coffee, to wake up. If first thing in the morning is your only available time, then I recommend taking at least a few minutes to wake up a bit. Remember, mindfulness meditation is mental training, and you're not going to be at your best if you're groggy.

You probably already have a good idea as to when you're the most alert, but it may not be the most feasible time. Considering all your commitments, you may need to determine the next best time. This can be a challenge, because most of us simply don't have spare time. If you're having trouble finding time to meditate, you may want to review your list of commitments from Step 3 to determine which are the most important.

Finding the time to meditate may just be a matter of good time management. I know there are times in my day when I'm simply wasting time, all the while thinking that I'm relaxing or unwinding. In reality, I may be doing neither. I sometimes engage in fruitless activities that are only agitating my mind.

I can often find time to dedicate to something by finding a few minutes here and there. If I look hard enough, I can come up with at least thirty minutes to meditate. This is no longer a problem for me because I know that mindfulness meditation makes me more productive, so it's high on my list of priorities.

You also need to consider the availability of quiet time. Various sounds in the background can be distracting, such as people talking, traffic, and barking dogs. I normally meditate late at night, when most people in the neighborhood are asleep. However, if I wait too long before starting my session, I may be too tired.

You may live in a busy household where there is a lot of activity. Determine which time of the day is quiet enough. This may be in the morning when everyone is still asleep, or later at night when most have gone to bed. There may even be a time when everyone is away from the house.

Another possibility is to ask the members of your household for some quiet time. Explain to them that you're trying to meditate, and you need the house to be as quiet as possible for a few minutes. Who knows, they may even consider joining you sometime. You'd be setting a good example for them to follow.

## Finding a Place Free of Distractions

Next, you want to find a place to meditate. Ideally, it would be a place that you could devote solely to your meditation practice. Your place of meditation is your sanctuary, where you can take the time to reconnect with your True Nature, and replenish your inner strength. This will help you stay committed to your practice.

You also want a place that is free of distractions, where you won't be disturbed during your meditation session. We've already talked about how

> Your place of meditation is your sanctuary, where you can take the time to reconnect with your True Nature, and replenish your inner strength.

noise can make it tough to meditate, but there are other types of distractions. They are usually sensory in nature. In other words, anything that stimulates any of your five senses can be a distraction, such as sounds, smells, sights, and anything that touches our body while we're meditating. All of these will trigger thoughts and keep your mind stimulated.

Strong smells, such as perfumes and cooking, can also be distracting. If this is the case, try ventilating the room before you begin your session. Incense can be a good solution because not only does it take care of the smell, but it can also set the mood and serve as a reminder of your meditation goals. If you use an air freshener, try to avoid using aerosol sprays, as they can give you a headache, and they're also not good for the environment.

Sights can also be distracting. They may not be much of a problem when you're meditating with your eyes closed, but they can be distracting if you are doing walking meditation. To give you some idea of how distracting they can be, I want to share a little experience that I had.

One day, I was doing walking meditation in my office, and I had several work-related items scattered about. At certain times during the session, I had a hard time staying focused on my footsteps. I kept thinking about work. At other times, staying focused seemed much easier. Then I realized that the times when I had trouble concentrating were when the work-related items came into view, and I had no trouble when the items were out of view. So just be aware that visual stimuli can affect your meditation session.

The sense of touch can be another source of mental stimulation. You obviously want to be comfortable when you're meditating, so wear clothes that are soft and loose-fitting. I know for me, comfortable clothing is important.

Of course, this discussion wouldn't be complete without some mention of the sense of taste. Believe it or not, having a strong aftertaste in your mouth can be distracting. You don't necessarily have to make brushing your teeth part of your meditation routine. It may suffice to simply rinse your mouth right before you start meditating.

If you usually eat just before meditating, then you have another issue to be concerned about; your blood sugar level. A spike in your blood sugar can make you feel anxious, sometimes to the point of feeling like you're having an anxiety attack. This problem is easily resolved with a few minutes of walking meditation, or some other form of light exercise.

Some meditation accessories may help you in your practice, such as incense, a mindfulness bell, or a lotus flower. They won't necessarily help you focus, but they will serve as reminders of your meditation goals. They also help in marking your meditation space.

I know some of you like listening to soothing music when meditating. While music can help you calm down, it can only get you to a certain point, and then it becomes an obstacle because it keeps stimulating your mind. If you want to listen to music during your meditation, I recommend using it just for a few minutes at the beginning of your session to help you calm down. Then turn it off so you can focus on concentration, or mindfulness. Once you gain some experience with the practice, I suggest dropping the music during your meditation sessions.

## Choosing a Sitting Position

Proper sitting position is another important element of your meditation practice. I'm sure you've seen pictures of people sitting on the floor with their legs crossed and their hands on their knees with palms up. That is actually a yoga meditation position. In mindfulness meditation, we do things a little differently. Our main objective is to find a sitting position that is comfortable and conducive to mental alertness.

You have two basic choices, either sitting on the floor on a meditation cushion with your legs crossed, or sitting in a chair. In either case, sit in such a way that your back is straight because you want to be able to breathe easily. If you're hunched over, then you'll start getting short of breath.

The three most common positions for sitting on a cushion are the Burmese style, half lotus, and full lotus:

- In the Burmese style, both legs lie flat on the floor from knee to foot parallel with each other.

- In the half lotus position, both knees touch the floor and one foot rests on the calf of the other leg.

- In the full lotus position, both knees touch the floor and each foot rests on the other leg's thigh.

Don't worry if you have physical limitations that preclude you from sitting on the floor. Sitting in a chair is perfectly fine. It is preferable to use one without arm rests, as they can get in the way of your hand position. Also, choose one that doesn't dig into the underside of your legs, as this can pinch the nerves in your legs and cause pain. Sit with your feet flat on the floor and with your back straight.

You'll have to experiment with these different positions, and choose the one that is most comfortable for you. The main objective is to find a position where you're relaxed and sitting up straight. You also want to be comfortable enough to sit in that position for your entire meditation session.

With regard to hand position, some teachers have very strict guidelines, but I don't. I am more concerned about comfort and avoiding distractions, than I am about symbolism, or anything else. If you're distracted by discomfort, then it will be harder to meditate. I recommend choosing a hand position that is comfortable for you, such as your hands resting on your thighs, or interlaced in front of you.

## How Long Should I Meditate?

When you first start out, it may be difficult to sit still for more than five or ten minutes. That's not uncommon, but don't worry if that happens. It usually takes a few meditation sessions to work your way up to longer periods. You can do this by increasing the duration by a few minutes each session. How quickly you increase the duration depends on how agitated your mind is. If you use the techniques from Step 3 for calming your mind, you'll be able to sit still longer.

How long you meditate depends on your goals as a spiritual seeker. However, if you want to achieve any significant progress, then your goal should be about forty minutes to an hour a day. I know that sounds like a long time, especially considering your commitments. In addition, some of us have a nagging feeling that we could be doing something more productive with our time.

Remember, mindfulness meditation is mental training, whereby you'll learn how to make better use of your time, because you'll have a greater understanding of the conse-quences of your actions. You will become more effective and productive in everything you do.

> *"The price of discipline is always less than the pain of regret."*
>
> ~ NIDO QUBEIN

Studies have confirmed this, so there's a significant return on your time invested in meditation.

I know some people who meditate, but don't seem to make much progress. They seem restless and continue struggling with personal issues. I later come to find out that they only meditate once or twice a week for just a few minutes at a time. And when they don't see results, they begin looking for a new form of meditation. They're not going to make much progress using that approach. If they knew how to meditate properly, they would see immediate results and would dedicate more time to their practice. Once you start believing that results from medi-tation will come slowly, it becomes a self-fulfilling prophecy. Don't settle for mediocre results.

On the other hand, I know people who are dedicated to a daily medi-tation practice. They are committed to one form of meditation, and are consistent with it. These people are generally very kind, loving, and outgoing. They are friendly and pleasant to be around. I rarely hear of them being embroiled in personal dramas, or see them struggling with the same issues repeatedly.

Dedicated meditators usually have a positive outlook on life. To them, every problem has a solution, and they take the necessary steps to resolve them. So naturally, when you make the decision to practice daily, you'll see steady progress, and there's no limit to how much you can grow. Our limits are only self-imposed.

I should also point out that there's a significant difference between thirty minutes and an hour of meditation. There is even a difference between forty minutes and an hour. It is much like doing aerobic exercises. You can get some benefit with twenty minutes on the StairMaster or treadmill, but it takes at least forty minutes to increase your metabolism enough to stimulate the fat-burning process.

The longer you meditate, the more your mind has a chance to settle down into a calm and focused state. Whenever I meditate for an hour or more, by the end of the session I feel like I'm in the zone. And that feeling stays with me for a couple of days. Try it, and you'll see for yourself the difference it makes.

I personally dedicate forty minutes to an hour a day. And like many of you, I have commitments that demand a great deal of my time, such as work, volunteering, house chores, and more. I've made the commitment to daily meditation, because I fully understand the impact it has on the quality of my life, and continue to make significant progress—even after years of practice.

What I think is even more amazing is that the more skilled I become at the practice, the faster I progress. So I urge you to make the commitment. Once you incorporate meditation time into your daily routine, it will become much easier. In time, you'll be glad you did.

Now, some of you may be fortunate enough to have plenty of time on your hands. If you do, then there is nothing wrong with meditating more than an hour a day. There have been periods in my life where I meditated for two or three hours a day. I have also attended retreats where we meditated for about seven hours a day.

The benefits I derived from meditating for that long were tremendous. I was able to make years worth of progress in just a few days. I began to experience an entirely different state of consciousness. My emotions became much more stable, and I felt a love and compassion for other people that I had never felt before.

Of course, these hours of meditation were divided into shorter sessions. If you want to try this yourself, I recommend sessions of about one to one and a half hours long. This will allow your mind to settle down enough to develop good concentration and mindfulness. To make a long session easier, you can incorporate walking meditation to allow you to stretch your body and continue meditating.

You can try meditating for longer periods either on your own, at a retreat, or both. I recommend attending a retreat because of the benefit you'll gain from meditating with others who share the same interests as you. At a retreat, you will also have the benefit of receiving guidance from an experienced teacher. Just make sure the retreat is grounded in a sound meditation practice. I think that a retreat that teaches you the basics of mindfulness meditation is probably one of the most effective.

## Conclusion

As a serious meditator, you realize the importance of using proper techniques. In this step, you learned how to design an effective meditation practice that fits your lifestyle. We discussed when, where, and how long to meditate. We also discussed finding a sitting position that is suitable for you.

*"It does not matter how slowly you go as long as you do not stop."*

~ Confucius

These are all important elements of a good meditation practice, which will enable you to get more from your efforts. If you see results from each meditation session, then you'll remain committed and make steady progress in your spiritual development.

In Step 5, I will explain the mechanics of meditation, and walk you through a typical session, so you know exactly what to do. Later in the Steps, I'll share with you some powerful tools that will dramatically speed up your progress.

Now that you're gaining a solid understanding of what meditation is all about, you won't have to spend years trying figure it out, like I did. The results will be immediate, and you will finally realize all the benefits that meditation has to offer.

## Exercises

The following exercises are guidelines to help you structure your meditation session. They are flexible enough so that you can adapt them to your needs and means. Your meditation session doesn't have to be anything elaborate. In fact, simple is more practical.

**1. Choose the best time of the day for you to meditate.** Choose a time when you are alert and the distractions are at a minimum. This may be early or late in the day when members of your household are asleep, and there are fewer outside distractions.

**2. Find a place to meditate.** Choose a place that is quiet and free of distractions. You may also want to choose a place where you can set up your props. If you are fortunate enough to have a spare room, you can turn it into a meditation room.

**3. Choose the best sitting position for you.** Not all of us can sit on a meditation cushion because of various physical limitations. Sitting in a chair is fine. Choose a sitting position where you can sit with your back straight, so that you remain alert and your breathing is not impaired.

**4. Decide how long to dedicate to your meditation sessions.** Through good time management, most of us can find the time we need to meditate. Review your list of commitments from Step 3. Include your meditation practice in the list where you think it belongs according to priority. If there isn't enough time for all your commitments, you can eliminate the ones at the bottom, that is, the ones with low priority. Remember, how fast you progress in your spiritual development is directly proportional to the effort you put into your practice.

**5.  Acquire some props for your meditation area. (optional)** These can include a meditation cushion, mindfulness bell, candle or incense, and maybe even a small table on which to set them. These props can be useful reminders of your meditation goals. Visit our website for some ideas. Our partners carry full lines of meditation accessories to help you in your practice.

# STEP 5
## How to Meditate for Deeper Awareness

*Silence is a source of great strength.*

~ Lao Tzu

### Chapter Highlights

**Step 5**   *"In order to enhance our spiritual evolution, we made mindfulness meditation a regular practice."*

B ACK IN THE MID-'90S when I was learning how to meditate, there was little awareness about meditation. There were few books, and it was certainly not talked about in the mainstream media like it is today. Furthermore, knowledgeable teachers were hard to come by. My progress was slow, and I didn't know that I could achieve much better results if I knew how to apply good meditation techniques. But I kept meditating out of sheer determination.

However, many beginners aren't as determined as I was. If they don't see results quickly, then they lose their enthusiasm and soon quit meditating. Furthermore, without some level of proficiency with our observation skills, our observations will be tainted with old views and emotions, and we'll be unable to see the world with clarity. The result will be that we won't achieve the inner peace we're searching for.

Meditation is a lot easier than you might think, once you understand the proper techniques and how to apply them. In Step 5, I will first discuss how to deal with distractions, such as drowsiness and a wandering mind. It's important to be able to identify them early, so that they don't gain too much momentum, which makes them more difficult to overcome.

> *"In the silence of our hearts, God speaks of His love."*
> – MOTHER TERESA

Next, I will discuss the techniques for developing concentration and mindfulness. These skills are indispensable if you want to be able to observe the world with greater clarity. Then I'll show you how to incorporate walking meditation into your session, for when you are too agitated to sit still.

When we're done with this step, you'll have a good understanding of how to get more from your meditation practice. You will develop a much deeper awareness of the world, leading to wisdom and inner peace. This training will open up a world you never knew existed.

## How to Deal with Distractions

When you meditate, your mind will naturally begin to wander. This is normal. All of our distractions come in the form of one or more of the Five Hindrances. Remember them from Step 1?

1. **Sensual desire.** This is our desire to please our five senses and emotions. During our meditation, desire manifests itself into fantasies. They can appear in the form of greed, lust, gluttony, or anything else that gives us sensual pleasure and emotional gratification.

2. **Aversion.** This is the opposite of sensual desire. It's natural for us to want to avoid unpleasant things. Aversion manifests itself into emotions, such as anger, jealousy, and resentment. It can also manifest itself into ill will, anger, and resentment.

3. **Lethargy.** This is a mental dullness that arises from boredom, or lack of mental stimulation. Many of us have an aversion to boredom. When we're bored, our mind begins to shut down by going into sleep mode.

4. **Agitation.** This is essentially the opposite of lethargy. It is the over-stimulation of our mind. When we're involved in too many activities, our thoughts gain so much momentum that it becomes difficult to slow down our mind. Agitation manifests itself into restlessness and worry. When we don't have something constructive to think about, then our thinking becomes destructive, as is the case with worrying.

5. **Doubt.** This is a lack of conviction and trust. It mainly refers to doubt about the effectiveness of our meditation practice.

When we have this kind of doubt, we begin just going through the motions in our practice, and the lack of effectiveness becomes a self-fulfilling prophecy.

Many people think that if they don't keep their mind completely focused, then they're not meditating properly. That is simply not so. It takes practice to develop concentration. What you're looking for is progress, not perfection.

So how do we overcome the Five Hindrances? Remember from Step 1, we're going to stand watch, like the police officer waiting for the speeding motorist to drive by. The idea is to identify each hindrance as it arises. Observe when it arises and when it dissipates. In other words, you're going to be very mindful of the hindrances, and not give them any more power by indulging them. By observing them this way, you are accomplishing three things:

- You are taking away their power, so they will diminish faster.
- You are developing mindfulness by observing them.
- You are getting to know yourself better.

With lethargy, you have to be especially mindful because it can gain momentum very quickly; and before you know it, you're falling asleep. In the beginning of your practice, it's important that you learn how to identify the hindrances when they arise. After some practice, you'll see which ones arise most frequently during your meditation, and you'll be able to identify them without calling them by name, and just be mindful of them. By practicing this way, you'll begin to remove the obstacles of your meditation, and you'll develop concentration and mindfulness much faster.

Over time, the hindrances will become less of a nuisance, and you'll be able to concentrate much better. Think of the implications to your daily life:

- You'll be able to concentrate better on job functions—helping you advance your career.

- Your personal relationships will improve, because you'll be able to pay closer attention to loved ones when you're interacting with them.

- You'll grow faster because you'll see how the hindrances manifest themselves in your life, which will lead to overcoming unwholesome habits.

On occasion, you will completely drift off in your thoughts, or become very sleepy. Don't beat yourself up when this happens. This is normal. If it didn't happen, then we'd all be enlightened. When you realize that you've drifted off, simply return to what you were doing; either concentrating on your breathing or observing it mindfully.

I find walking meditation to be a useful tool for dealing with lethargy. It's difficult to fall asleep when you're walking. I've heard of people falling asleep while standing, but not while walking. We'll talk more about walking meditation shortly.

## Training Your Mind to Concentrate

In the beginning of our practice, we're going to place more emphasis on developing concentration. Since concentration is a bit more challenging to develop than mindfulness, there's a tendency to neglect it, and simply focus on mindfulness. It is easier to simply observe our stray thoughts than to keep our attention focused on one object.

> By staying focused on your breathing, you keep yourself anchored in the present moment.

If you neglect concentration training, then your mindfulness will be superficial, and you'll be unable to look deeply into the object of your meditation. With a good balance of concentration and mindfulness, you'll be able to see beyond the surface, and gain much greater insight.

Concentration is similar to mindfulness in that you're paying attention to something. However, it is different in the sense that you're trying to focus all your attention on just one object. When practicing mindfulness, you're not excluding anything; you're being aware of what is happening in the present moment. I guess you can say that concentration is forced mindfulness. The reason you will practice both is that each one will help you develop the other.

So how do you practice concentration during your meditation? Simply pick an object on which to concentrate and stay with it. Your breath is usually the best object for this training, because it is the easiest thing to observe with your eyes closed. By staying focused on your breathing, you keep yourself anchored in the present moment, because that is where your breathing is always taking place.

Now, staying focused on your breathing might sound simple, but it's not always easy. The good news is that there's a technique that will help you maintain your concentration. This technique is counting. In the beginning of your practice, some stray thoughts will interrupt your meditation, but counting will help you maintain your concentration. You can use various counting schemes, but start with counting your breaths one through five silently in your mind. When you get to five, simply start over again. When a distraction arises during your meditation, just ignore it and immediately bring your attention back to your breath.

Concentrate on the sensation of the air passing through the tip of your nose. It is much easier to focus on one particular aspect of our breathing than to focus on the entire breathing function. That we'll do when the objective of our meditation is to develop mindfulness. I prefer counting on the out-breath. You may find it easier to count on the in-breath. Do whichever is easiest for you.

There is one thing to be aware of when counting your breathing: you may catch yourself simply counting, and not concentrating of your breathing. You can easily overcome this problem by changing the counting scheme, such as 1-4, 1-6, or 1-10. By changing it up, you'll force yourself to pay closer attention.

## Developing Insight through Mindfulness Training

Now let's talk about practicing mindfulness during your meditation. Again, the object of your meditation will be your breath. However, instead of counting each one, simply observe it without forcing yourself, like you did when practicing concentration.

Begin by observing the sensation of the air entering your nostrils, going down your windpipe, and into your lungs. Then observe the expansion and contraction of your lungs with each breath. Finally, turn your attention to the entire breath as one continuous graceful motion. As you develop concentration and mindfulness, you'll begin to notice more of the subtle actions your body is performing during the breathing process.

Remember, with mindfulness your attention is not fixed on one object. It is more of a gentle observation of what is taking place. This means that you are more relaxed, and not forcing yourself to do something. You may find that distracting thoughts, in the form of the Five Hindrances, will enter your mind with much greater ease. When a distraction arises, observe it as it comes into being, then gently watch it slip away without clinging to it.

In the beginning of your practice, it is usually best to start your meditation sessions with the concentration techniques. When your mind calms down after a few minutes, then you can switch over to practicing mindfulness. I recommend that you start out by spending about three-quarters of your session practicing concentration, and the last quarter on mindfulness. By doing this, those last few minutes will be more mindful than if you simply started your session with mindfulness.

## Meditation Formats

There are three basic formats for your meditation session you can choose from. With these, you'll be able to add variety to your practice, so that you continue getting joy and fulfillment, and making steady progress:

- Begin with a focus on concentration, then switch to mindfulness.
- Focus mainly on practicing mindfulness.
- Alternate between concentration and mindfulness.

With the first format, begin your session with the objective of establishing concentration. Use the breath as the object of your concentration, using one of the counting schemes described above. Once you've steadied your mind, switch over to mindfulness meditation. Drop the counting and just observe your entire breath mindfully.

> Eventually, distractions will dissipate and your mind will become more calm, focused, and alert.

I recommend using this format predominantly in the beginning of your practice because it will help you place more emphasis on concentration. As you progress and are able to establish concentration more quickly, you can switch over to the mindfulness portion of your session sooner. However, keep in mind that you're not trying to eliminate the need for concentration altogether. Both concentration and mindfulness will always be equally important to our practice, because each will continue to aid in the development of the other.

The second format is pretty straightforward, but a bit harder to practice if you are restless and agitated. Begin your meditation session using mindfulness, by maintaining awareness of the entire breathing process. When a hindrance arises, observe it as it arises and when it dissipates. Then relax and return your attention to your breath, observing all its nuances. As you practice this way, your concentration and mindfulness will deepen. Eventually, distractions will dissipate and your mind will become more calm, focused, and alert.

In the third format, you will begin with either concentration or mindfulness, and switch back and forth as the need arises. If you begin with concentration, you may have difficulty keeping your mind focused on your breath, and start getting restless and frustrated. What you would do then is switch over to mindfulness, and observe those feelings of frustration and restlessness.

Once your mind has steadied a bit, switch back over to concentration and try to maintain your focus on your breath, while ignoring stray thoughts that may arise. By practicing this way, both your concentration and mindfulness will deepen, and you'll be able to observe the object of your meditation at a much deeper level without being distracted.

There are times when you may want to practice only concentration, and other times when you want to practice only mindfulness during a particular session. The idea is to get some extra practice to improve both these observation skills. So feel free to change things up.

Pay special attention to the difference between concentration and mindfulness. It is easy to overlook the difference early in your practice, and if you're not sure which one you are practicing, then you may be practicing neither. I suggest you dedicate a few sessions to using the third format, switching back and forth between the two, and paying close attention to the difference between them. Remember that with concentration, you're forcing yourself to pay attention to your breath, and with mindfulness, you're observing it gently. It is important to learn the difference.

In time, your concentration and mindfulness skills will begin working together, and your development will start progressing faster. It is much like a runner who is training for a race. As he becomes more proficient with the basic running techniques, he will be able to run faster and farther. So you too will be able to travel the path to enlightenment faster, and go much farther.

## Let's Meditate Together

You now have the tools necessary for an effective and productive meditation session. I will guide you through a meditation session, so you understand how to apply them. So, get out your meditation props, such as incense or a candle, turn the lights down, and get into your meditation position. Here are a few things you can do to help get into the right frame of mind:

> One truly mindful breath can go a long way toward enlightenment.

**Establish your personal time.** Give yourself permission to set aside all your concerns while you're meditating. For the next few minutes, you don't have to think about friends, associates, or loved ones. This is your personal time to dedicate to your spiritual development. Put all other commitments on hold, and don't worry about anything left undone. You can return to them when you're finished meditating.

**Establish the objective of your meditation session.** That is, what do you want to accomplish? Are you going to focus on concentration or mindfulness? Let's start with the first format described above. Since we'll focus on concentration, make a relentless effort to keep your attention fixed on the object of your meditation—the breath. When a distraction arises during concentration meditation, simply ignore it and return to your breath. When a distraction arises during mindfulness meditation, identify the hindrance and watch it dissipate.

**Cultivate compassion for others.** This helps me open my heart and tap into my own True Nature, which is exactly where I want to go through my meditation. Think about the people in your life who may be going through difficulties, and cultivate compassion for their suffering. You can also cultivate compassion for people you may not know personally, who may be suffering. Do which ever gets you into a more loving and compassionate frame of mind.

## Let's Begin...

- If you have a mindfulness bell, begin your meditation session with three sounds of the bell. Otherwise, begin with three deep breaths.

- Gently close your eyes and begin counting each breath silently in your mind, one through five. Focus your attention on the sensation of the air passing through the tip of your nose. You can count either on the in-breath, or on the out-breath. Do whichever is most comfortable for you.

- When a stray thought or outside distraction interrupts your concentration, simply ignore it and immediately bring your attention back to you breath.

- Stop counting about three-quarters of the way through your session, and change your focus over to mindfulness. That is, simply observe your breath mindfully.

- Notice the sensation the air makes entering your nose, then passing through your windpipe, and then entering your lungs. Observe how your lungs expand with each in-breath, and contract with each out-breath.

- As you practice mindfulness, simply observe the entire breathing process. Don't focus on any one aspect of your breath, but rather maintain awareness that your breathing is taking place.

- When a distraction arises, ask yourself: is this sensual desire, aversion, agitation or worry, lethargy, or doubt? When you have identified it, simply watch it pass without indulging or clinging to it.

- When you reach the end of your session, invite the bell three times, or simply open your eyes gently and bring your awareness back to your surroundings. Feel free to stretch your legs, or any other part of your body that needs stretching.

How did you do? Did you have any difficulty staying focused? Don't worry if you did. In fact, look at it the other way around. Was there a time during your session when you were truly concentrated, or mindful of your breath? If so, then consider it a success. This is a success you can build on. Remember, just one truly mindful breath can go a long way toward enlightenment.

## Walking Your Way to Mindfulness

Walking meditation is another form of meditation that is commonly practiced in Buddhism. It's great for developing concentration without getting bored. You can use the same techniques and formats that you use in sitting meditation. The only difference now is that you perform them while walking. With walking meditation, you will walk much slower than usual.

Mindful walking has a very strong calming effect. There are two reasons for this. First, it challenges your sense of balance. If you have to pay close attention to keeping your balance, then you force yourself to concentrate and be mindful, and therefore, stay in the present moment. Second, by slowing down your body, you force your mind to follow.

If you want to practice concentration with walking meditation, then focus your attention on just one aspect of the walking motion, such as the sensation on the bottom of your feet as you take each step. Incorporate one of the counting schemes described above. When your mind goes astray, bring it back immediately and continue counting your footsteps.

If you want to practice mindfulness with walking meditation, then gently observe all the parts of your body that are involved in the walking motion, such as your feet, calves, thighs, hips, and shoulders. What other parts of your body are involved? Notice the way they move, and how they all work together to perform one graceful motion. How about your balance? What's involved in keeping your balance?

When any of the hindrances arise, deal with them in the same manner as during sitting meditation. Then bring your attention back to your footsteps. As you can see, you can learn so much about your body by walking mindfully.

I usually incorporate walking meditation into my meditation session. I'll begin with about 10-15 minutes of walking meditation, and then do about forty minutes of sitting meditation. This serves several functions:

- It helps my mind settle down. By walking slowly, I force my mind to slow down.

- It keeps my body from getting uncomfortable from sitting for long periods.

- It helps me burn off any excess sugar that may be in my bloodstream, which can make me feel restless or anxious.

You can use walking meditation in different ways:

- At the beginning of your session, as I've just described, to help you ease into your meditation.

- In the middle, to ease some of the discomfort from sitting for a long time.

- At the end, to also help ease some of the discomfort from sitting. It can help on those occasions when you may have difficulty sitting still for whatever reason.

Sometimes, I will even do a whole session of walking meditation. This can be very calming if you do it outside in a beautiful setting, such as a park or garden. In addition to being mindful of your footsteps, be mindful of your surroundings. Enjoy the beauty and wonders of nature, such as the trees, flowers, fresh air, and all the critters.

## Conclusion

Congratulations! You now know how to meditate like a monk. You can now meditate with confidence, knowing that you'll make steady progress. In this step, you learned the mechanics of an effective meditation session. You learned how to practice concentration and mindfulness, and how to deal with distractions as they arise. Practicing this way may seem a little challenging at first, but I assure you that it'll get much easier as your mind settles down, and you're better able to recognize distractions.

These techniques are important to your meditation practice because they will help you develop mental discipline, which is essential to your spiritual growth. Your thinking and actions will become proactive, instead of reactive. You will be able to determine the direction of your life, instead of letting your emotions do it for you.

In the next step, you'll learn how to monitor your progress, so that you stay motivated and committed to your practice. Later in the steps, I'll share with you some valuable tips for speeding up your progress. That's when it really gets interesting. Soon you will develop a level of mindfulness that will forever transform your life. Then dealing with life's difficulties will become much easier. I wish somebody had taught me these techniques when I was first learning how to meditate. It would have saved me a lot of time and effort, and a lot of pain and suffering.

## Exercises

The following exercises will help you develop your meditation techniques. In the beginning of your practice, place more emphasis on developing concentration. Once you gain some experience, seek a more even balance between concentration and mindfulness. As you develop your ability to identify the hindrances more quickly, your proficiency with these observation skills will increase. These exercises will also help you evaluate your initial experiences, so you can make any adjustments where necessary.

**1. Begin meditating using the first format described earlier.** Begin your meditation sessions with one of the counting schemes to help you stay focused on your breath, in particular, the sensation of air passing through the tip of your nose. It may be a challenge at first, but make a relentless effort to keep your attention on this spot. About three-quarters of the way through your session, stop counting and begin observing the entire breathing process with mindfulness. Remember that mindfulness is a gentle awareness of what is happening.

**2.   Become familiar with the Five Hindrances.** Awareness of them will help you tremendously in diminishing their disruption of your meditation, and your life in general. Practice identifying them during your meditation sessions, and in your daily activities. Observe when they arise, and when they dissipate. In your notebook, make a note of which hindrances arise most frequently during your meditation, and in your life.

**3.   Observe the difference between concentration and mindfulness.** This is often a source of confusion for many people. Describe in your own words your understanding of both concentration and mindfulness. Then observe the difference between the two during your meditation.

**4.   Incorporate walking meditation into your practice.** It can add variety to your meditation session, while still practicing concentration and mindfulness. It will also enable you to meditate longer. Try walking meditation for about 10-15 minutes at the beginning of your meditation session. Also try a whole session of walking meditation in a quiet setting, such as a park, garden, or just around your neighborhood. Remember to be mindful of the beautiful surroundings.

**5.   As you progress in your practice, begin to focus more on mindfulness in your meditation sessions.** However, do not get away from practicing concentration altogether, as it is essential to your development of deeper mindfulness.

**6.   Evaluate your meditation sessions.** After each of your first few sessions, write down your observations. Answer the following questions, and make any necessary adjustments:

- Was your environment adequate?
- Was the time of day suitable?
- Which hindrances kept coming up?
- Did you have any periods of good concentration or mindfulness?
- How did you feel immediately after meditating?
- How did you feel in the days following your meditation?
    » Was your mind more calm, focused, and steady?
    » Were you more emotionally stable?
    » Did you gain any new insights?
    » How did you feel about yourself, and other people?

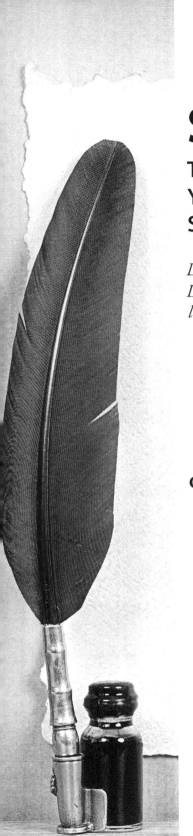

# STEP 6

## The Meditation Journal: Your Tool for Making Steady Progress

*Drop by drop is the water pot filled.
Likewise, the wise man, gathering it
little by little, fills himself with good.*

~ Buddha

### Chapter Highlights

- Staying Focused and Motivated with a Meditation Journal
- How to Keep a Journal: Setting Goals and Measuring Your Progress
- Reviewing Your Journal: See How Much You've Grown
- Double Entry Format for Deeper Insight
- Conclusion
- Exercises

**Step 6**   *"We remained vigilant in our meditation practice, so that we continued making steady progress."*

MANY PEOPLE START A MEDITATION practice with good intentions and lots of enthusiasm, but few of them stay committed long-term. They meditate regularly for a while, but soon lose interest when they stop seeing results from their efforts. I know this from personal experience.

When I was learning, I simply assumed that I was making progress, even though I really didn't see much result from my practice. I later realized that one of the reasons I saw few results was because the changes felt natural. I thought I had remained the same person when, in fact, I was changing all the time.

While it's good that you may be growing despite not seeing your progress, in time you will lose your enthusiasm, and have a hard time staying committed to your practice. When that happens, you'll slowly cut back on your meditation, and eventually quit. Then all your pain and suffering will return.

A meditation journal is an effective tool for monitoring your progress. By keeping track of how you feel, you will clearly see the changes in your demeanor and personality. You'll be able to see how you remain calm in tense situations, such as when you're in traffic or in the checkout line at the store. You will also see how you're no longer easily provoked by other people.

There are a couple of additional benefits of keeping a meditation journal. First, it will help you develop mindfulness. By actively examining your changing perceptions and emotions, you will train yourself to look deeper into the causes of your suffering. Second, the journal will help you improve your use of the meditation techniques, which will speed up your spiritual development.

In this step, I'll show you how to use a meditation journal to set goals in your practice, and monitor your progress as you achieve them. You will learn how to track both short-term and long-term results. You will see for yourself that a meditation journal can go a long way toward helping you stay committed to your practice.

## Staying Focused and Motivated with a Meditation Journal

Sometimes, your progress can be hard to see, even if it's significant. The changes will seem natural, and it may not be obvious that they're the direct result of your meditation practice. To give you an example: at one point in my development, I began to get less and less irritated while driving, but I didn't notice it at first because we usually notice things when they bother us, rather than when they don't bother us. It's kind of like not having a toothache. How many of you are aware that you don't have a toothache right now? You probably didn't notice it until I mentioned it, because not having a toothache is natural. Our spiritual development is very similar.

> A meditation journal will make it easier for you to stay focused and moving forward.

If you cannot see your progress, then it will become easy to get distracted from your practice, and you'll lose the benefits you've gained so far. A meditation journal will make it easier for you to stay focused and moving forward. It will help you in several ways:

**Establish goals for the upcoming week or month.** This will help you stay focused on your practice because you will have a plan of action.

**Ensure that you're accomplishing your goals.** You can see if your concentration and mindfulness are improving, and if the hindrances are dissipating. This will help you stay motivated.

**Identify your strengths and weaknesses.** You'll be able to see which of the Five Hindrances are most common in your meditation. If you spot a weakness, then you can work on overcoming it. I know that with some skills, it's acceptable to improve your strengths and ignore your weaknesses. Mindfulness meditation is not a practice where we can specialize in one particular technique. If you don't become proficient with all the techniques of the practice, then you will stop making steady progress toward your goal of achieving inner peace. In other words, your weaknesses will become obstacles to your spiritual development. Becoming aware of them is the starting point.

**Develop strategies for overcoming your weaknesses.** Once you're aware of your weaknesses, you can develop a plan for overcoming them. For example, if you're having a problem with a particular hindrance, you may want to look at it more closely. That is, look at the views associated with that hindrance, so you can gain a deeper insight into its cause. I think you'll find that by practicing diligently, the hindrances will gradually dissipate.

**Identify patterns and trends over time.** As you add variation to your practice, you'll be able to see which formats are yielding the best results for you. You can then make any necessary adjustments. These trends are almost impossible to spot if you're not keeping some form of written record.

**Stay motivated because you'll clearly see how you're growing.** This is probably the most exciting benefit of keeping a journal. As you practice diligently, you'll begin to see dramatic changes in yourself. Through your written journal, your progress will become self-evident.

## How to Keep a Journal: Setting Goals and Measuring Your Progress

There are various ways of keeping a journal. Some people like a checklist format. I don't really like this format because it's easy to go through the checklist without reflecting on your experience. It also doesn't capture some of the subtle changes that are taking place. I prefer a freestyle format where you can write freely about your experiences, but at the same time, you need some structure so that it's easy to review later.

In the next two sections, we'll look at some important entries that will help you get the most out of your meditation journal. They are classified into two basic types of entries; formal and informal.

## Formal Entries

When keeping a journal, it is necessary to make some formal entries. These entries will make it easier to track your progress, and the reasons. They include:

- Date and time of meditation session
- Duration of session
- Focus on concentration or mindfulness
- Sitting and/or walking meditation
- Goal of your meditation session

When making these entries, there's no need to elaborate, unless you feel it's necessary for some reason. You may need to elaborate on your goals because they can vary significantly. Make your goals forward-looking, and establish them at the beginning of the week, or at another time you may find more suitable. Here are some ideas:

- Do you want to focus on concentration or mindfulness, or some combination?
- Do you want to focus on learning to identify the Five Hindrances?
- Do you want to emphasize mindfulness of the hindrances?
- Do you want to increase the duration of your sessions? For example, in the upcoming week, you can try increasing the duration by five or ten minutes at a time.
- Do you want to focus on learning the techniques?

I suggest you pay special attention to the use of proper techniques during your meditation sessions. For example, you can dedicate several sessions to learning a specific technique, such as identifying the Five Hindrances. Or, if you're having difficulty with concentration, you can make it a goal to focus on that.

In the beginning of my practice, I had difficulty maintaining concentration on my breath. I would sometimes catch myself simply counting, thinking I was concentrating when, in fact, I was just drifting. I had to make a special effort to identify concentration, and also mindfulness.

It's easy to take some of the techniques for granted, and then realize sometime down the road that we're getting lax in our practice. Remember, the better your techniques are, the faster you will grow. So, go ahead and use some of these seemingly simple techniques as the goals of your meditation sessions. In fact, I recommend that you regularly make it a goal to learn proper techniques. Otherwise, you run the risk of developing bad habits, and compromising your hard-earned spiritual growth.

## Informal Entries

Now let's look at some of the more informal entries. Here you can write freestyle to capture some of the nuances of your observations. This will help you make more sense of your experiences. I would suggest highlighting some keywords as you go along, because it will save you time later when you want to review past journal entries. You won't have to read an entire paragraph to determine what it's about.

> There will be times when you feel the whole world is beginning to make more sense.

You can write about a vast number of things in your informal journal entries. We each progress at a different pace, so everyone's journal will be unique. At the same time, there are some general observations you may want to include in your entries:

- What was happening in your life on the day of your meditation session? These factors can include the amount of sleep you've been getting, your diet (especially sugar intake), and stressful situations. Did you have a busy schedule? Were you dealing with any particular emotions or family issues?

- Which hindrances kept distracting you, and how well were you dealing with them?

- How was your meditation environment? Was it quiet, or noisy? Were there any outside distractions? Maybe you need to make some adjustments, such as the time and place.

- How did your meditation feel? Were you peaceful, or restless?

- How well were you able to accomplish your goals?

- Is your use of the techniques getting easier?

- Did you have any moments of deep concentration or mindfulness? How did you achieve these moments? Can you recreate them?

- How did you feel the rest of the day? Did you feel any different than before?

- Have you gained some new and interesting insights about yourself, or the world?

- You especially want to write about how you've changed over the last few days, or weeks.

This last item may be a bit more challenging to identify. It is like looking for the non-toothache; the things that are no longer there, such as behaviors, habits, and views that aren't serving you well. It can also be your general demeanor:

- Are you calmer, or more focused?

- Are you no longer reacting to things that used to provoke you?

- Do you treat people differently?

These are all changes that you will experience, but you may not notice them because they'll seem natural, and you may not associate them with being the result of your meditation practice.

Some of your experiences may be new to you, so you may not yet fully understand them. Writing about them will help you reflect on those experiences, and what your practice had to do with them.

You may also experience an epiphany. In fact, there will be times when you feel the whole world is beginning to make more sense. It is wonderful when this happens. As you continue practicing, you will certainly experience them more often.

There are three main factors that can trigger an epiphany. The first is that you are stimulating deeper parts of your brain, mainly your subconscious mind. By calming your mind, you're clearing it of unnecessary traffic, and therefore, you're able to access more of your memory. Your subconscious mind can remember things that our conscious mind cannot. That knowledge has been there for some time, but you just don't remember it being there. This is why your memory will improve through the practice of mindfulness meditation.

The second factor is that you're awakening your True Nature. You're beginning to perceive the world with another sense—a sixth sense—and tap into a universal consciousness that you weren't aware existed.

The third factor is simply mindfulness. As you develop your observation skills, you'll be able to see the interconnectedness of the whole world. You'll be able to see the cause and effect of different phenomena with much greater clarity. You'll begin to see your connection with the rest of humanity, and realize that your welfare and that of others are interdependent. This is the fruit of concentration and mindfulness. It is wisdom beginning to emerge in you, and when this happens, you'll begin to see the importance of passing it onto others.

## Reviewing Your Journal: See How Much You've Grown

Reviewing your journal regularly will help you develop mindfulness because you'll gain greater awareness of yourself, and how you're progressing. Here are some of the benefits of reviewing your journal:

- You will stay motivated because you'll clearly see the progress you're making.

- You will be able to identify trends. It's impossible to spot trends from just a couple of journal entries, but you can see them if you look at several past entries.

- You will be able to identify strengths or weaknesses. You may see some shortcomings that were not readily apparent when you were making the entries. This will help you identify things that you may need to work on, that is, future goals.

- You will correlate the changes in you with your meditation practice.

I recommend that you review your journal at least every other week; once a week is even better. This will help you look at your experiences from a different perspective, and you'll likely spot things you didn't notice before, such as changes and trends.

*"You don't need to be better than anyone else. You just need to be better than you used to be."*

~ Wayne W. Dyer

I would also recommend you review your journal over longer periods of time, such as three months, six months, or even a year. The reason is that by then you will have developed much deeper insight, so your perspective will be clearer. It's like looking at your childhood, but with the wisdom of a mature adult. You'll be able to understand yourself much better, and see how your old thinking and behavior may not be serving you well.

## Double Entry Format for Deeper Insight

There is a variation of the freestyle format that I really like. It is the double entry format. With this format, you make your entries on every other page, such as the right page of your notebook. When you do your weekly review, make notes of further reflections of your entries on the left page. You may notice something particularly interesting, spot a trend, or simply summarize your entry in a sentence or two. This will help you when you do a review over a longer period of time, such as three or six months.

## Conclusion

As you can see, keeping a meditation journal is easy and the benefits are tremendous, especially if you're just getting started in your practice. By writing down your experiences, you'll be able to stay committed and keep the momentum moving forward. This makes the journal an indispensable tool for maintaining progress toward your spiritual goals.

*"The way you think, the way you behave, the way you eat, can influence your life by 30 to 50 years."*

~ DEEPAK CHOPRA

Now that you understand the basics of mindfulness meditation, it's time for some more advanced techniques. Next, I'll share with you a variety of tools that will enhance your practice. You will learn how to put the Three Jewels into practice, which will significantly speed up your development.

You have now reached a fork in the road. The time has come to make a decision that will impact the rest of your life. Those who remain diligent and committed to their practice will surely find peace, and those who don't will remain caught up in their suffering. You have the choice between settling for your current situation, and pursuing true enlightenment. It takes courage and determination to continue on this spiritual path. I hope you will stay with me on this journey of self-discovery.

## Exercises

The following exercises will help you get started with your meditation journal. They are designed to help you stay engaged and committed to your practice by setting goals, and keeping track of your progress.

**1. Begin keeping a meditation journal:**

a. **Make the formal entries** such as date, time, duration, and goal of meditation sessions.

b. **Write about your successes.** For example, are you able to concentrate for longer periods of time without being distracted? Is your mindfulness getting deeper? Are you gaining a better understanding of the techniques?

c. **Write about your challenges.** Which hindrances come up most often? Are you having trouble understanding the difference between concentration and mindfulness? Are you having trouble with a particular technique? If you're experiencing such challenges, it would be a good idea to review the pertinent discussion in this book, and examine your application of the technique.

**2. Establish forward-looking goals for your meditation practice.** Goals will help you stay focused and keep you moving forward. If you wander off course, your progress will slow tremendously. Most of your goals should include developing concentration and mindfulness, even at intermediate and advanced levels of practice, as these are your primary tools of observation. Once you've developed them to some level of proficiency, you can begin applying them to different subjects of meditation, such as impermanence and interbeing.

**3. Review your journal periodically.** I recommend you review your journal at least every other week. It doesn't have to be an elaborate review. Just note some things that you didn't see before. Then do a more thoughtful review at three or six months. This will help you see patterns in your successes and challenges. Notice how your application of the techniques is improving, or where you may be wandering off course. Most importantly, look at how you are changing. Are you more stable emotionally? Are you more focused and insightful? Are you treating people with more loving-kindness?

**4.  Keep a close eye out for the amount of time you spend working on concentration.** This is an area that some people cut back on because it requires more effort, yet it is vital to your development. If you focus too much on just developing mindfulness without concentration, then your mindfulness will only be superficial. You'll be unable to see the roots of your suffering, and therefore, never achieve true freedom.

# STEP 7
## Discover the Power of Meditating with Others

*Thousands of candles can be lighted from a single candle, and the life of the single candle will not be shortened. Happiness never decreases by being shared.*

~ BUDDHA

## Chapter Highlights

- Mindfulness Energy: The Nourishment of Inner Peace and Wisdom
- Connecting with Other People to Enhance Your Practice
- Learning to Be More Sociable
- Wonderful People Are Everywhere!
- The Meditation Group: Your Spiritual Refuge
- Conclusion
- Exercises

**Step 7**   *"We became aware that other people can provide us with the spiritual nourishment vital to our development."*

CONGRATULATIONS! I ASSUME THAT SINCE you're still reading this book, you've made the decision to stay committed to your meditation practice. I think you've made the right choice. Your perseverance will be rewarded with peace, wisdom, and enlightenment. As my first mentor once told me, "You can give yourself one pat on the back."

When I was a young man, I was shy and had a hard time making friends. Like most other kids in school, I wanted to be popular, but found it impossible to develop any meaningful relationships. I felt lonely and disconnected from the rest of the world. It was a painful existence.

This is no longer the case. With some work and determination, and mindfulness, I learned how to connect with people on a meaningful level. Today, I literally have hundreds of friends who will come to my aid if needed. To a great extent, this is because I took the time to be there for them in their times of need.

Sociability has important implications to our spiritual development. Most of us want to have friends with whom we can share our joys and sorrows. We know that our lives are better when we have people we can connect with on an intimate level. After all, we are social creatures, and we need the strength from others to help us get through life.

While meditating alone is an important part of your practice, it would be difficult to make significant progress if you didn't meditate with others. You would be depriving yourself of valuable sources of spiritual nourishment that would significantly enhance your spiritual and emotional growth. Your progress would be slow, and you would have a hard time overcoming the wounds from your past, or any other emotional issues. You need the strength from others to help you grow.

Now that you know the basics of mindfulness meditation, I'm going to show you how to enhance your practice by getting involved in a sangha. In Step 2, we talked about the sangha, the spiritual community that supports your practice, but only in principle. Now I'm going to show you how to use it to help you grow faster.

In Step 7, you're going to learn how to connect with other people and participate in a sangha. These are essential components of your meditation practice. The great thing about connecting with others is that it will enrich your life tremendously. You will make many close friends with people who are kind and compassionate, and sincere about promoting peace and harmony. This is your chance to contribute to world peace, in addition to helping yourself.

## Mindfulness Energy: The Nourishment of Inner Peace and Wisdom

To fully appreciate the healing power of the sangha, it would help to understand what mindfulness energy is, and how it works. Remember that the energy of mindfulness is the energy of consciousness. It is the spiritual energy that shines the light on reality, and therefore, leads to wisdom and inner peace.

Our meditation practice is essentially raising our energy level and in doing so, we're able to see more clearly. It is much like a dimmer switch for the light in a room. As you turn the switch, you increase the amount of electricity passing through the circuit and into the light bulb, making it shine brighter. This makes it easier to see what is in the room.

We all radiate mindfulness energy and other people can sense it. For example, have you ever sensed a feeling of warmth and love radiating from someone in the room? There are two reasons why this happens. First, that person was indeed radiating mindfulness energy, either to everyone in the vicinity, or to us in particular. The person was obviously very open and loving. She was well along her spiritual path, and had a strong connection to her inner source of mindfulness energy, so she had plenty to share with others.

The second reason was that we were probably receptive to her. In other words, we were open and our attention was directed at her. Keep in mind that there are varying degrees of these two factors which determine how much mindfulness energy we receive. When practicing mindfulness meditation, not only are we trying to raise our own energy level, but we're also trying to be more open and receptive to others.

> Mindfulness is the energy of love, and the driving force behind all human relationships and interactions.

Now let me ask you this: have you ever sensed a dark feeling coming from a person in the room? It probably felt like the life was being drained from you. We usually get this effect from someone who is either very dominating, controlling, or needy. What is happening in this situation is similar to when a loving person is in the room, except the energy is flowing in the opposite direction.

This person has not yet learned to connect with sources of mindfulness energy in a healthy manner, and therefore, has to manipulate it from other people in order to feel at ease. Even though sometimes they might harm other people with their actions, they are not evil people. They are simply unmindful and spiritually weak.

I once knew a young lady who was very needy. She always saw herself as the victim of other people's injustices. She kept getting involved in abusive relationships, even to the point of being beaten by her boyfriend. When she was around other people, she was always afraid that they might say or do something that she couldn't handle. This created a tense atmosphere, like we were constantly walking on eggshells. It was exhausting because the energy kept flowing in her direction.

I've also known people who were dominating and controlling. One gentleman was the district manager in a chain of stores. He was used to giving orders to his employees who couldn't challenge his authority. When he was outside his work environment, he behaved exactly the same way. He expected his friends and associates to follow his orders; otherwise, he would get very upset. It was just as exhausting being around him as it was being around a needy person. Each had his own way of manipulating the energy out of other people.

Mindfulness is the energy of love, and the driving force behind all human relationships and interactions. We can share it freely, steal it, extort it, or convince people to give it to us willingly. This often leads to power struggles, which many of us engage in to some degree. That's because it isn't easy to tap directly into our True Nature to re-energize. However, this kind of behavior is unnecessary because the energy of mindfulness is plentiful, and more than enough to nurture everyone's spiritual development. We just need to learn how to access it.

This is where mindfulness meditation and the Three Jewels come in. By dwelling in the Three Jewels, we're able to connect with the three primary sources of mindfulness energy:

- When we dwell in the Buddha (our own Buddha Nature, or True Nature), we connect directly with the source of mindfulness energy.
- When we dwell in the Dharma, we use the spiritual principles to engage the flow of mindfulness energy.
- When we dwell in the Sangha, we connect with the Buddha Nature of other people.

Of the three, the Sangha is the easiest to engage. The Dharma takes some time to learn, and put into practice. Connecting with our Buddha Nature through our meditation practice also takes time as we develop our meditation skills. However, to dwell in the Sangha we basically just need to show up at the gatherings, and open our heart to other people.

I realize that for some of us, connecting with other people can be a challenge. It was extremely difficult for me when I was young, but I learned. Even without any social skills, I still benefited from simply showing up where people gathered to engage in some form of spiritual practice, or social activity.

## Connecting with Other People to Enhance Your Practice

While the Sangha is usually interpreted as our meditation group, the definition can be expanded to include other groups, and anyone we connect with on a meaningful level. This can include family, friends, and even strangers we encounter briefly through our daily activities. If we limit our Sangha to only the people we know, then we'll miss out on the enormous amount of spiritual nourishment available to us just about everywhere we go.

In some cultures, people are taught to trust only their family, and distrust everyone else. They can be very loving and thoughtful toward their own family, yet keep strangers at a distance. Sometimes they have difficulty making friends because they're not willing to open up to people outside their family. And if they have strained relationships with their family, then they're probably alone. Strangers are just as likely to be kind, or unkind, as our own family members. After all, aren't we strangers to people who don't know us?

It is possible to make deep spiritual connections with just about everyone we encounter. How well we connect with others mostly depends on how much we're willing and able to open our heart. Think about the last time you went to the store to buy something. While in the store, we're often preoccupied with other things we need to do, or with personal issues. We usually go in there and quickly get what we need, stand in line to pay, and then hurry back to do more important things than shopping.

Undoubtedly, there are many wonderful people at that store who are willing to interact with us, if only they were given a reason and an opportunity. Some of the people there are lonely, and need someone to talk with.

Let me ask you this: how would you react if someone at the store smiled at you and said some kind words, or complimented you on something? You would probably let your walls down a bit. Right? You might engage them in a short and pleasant conversation, and who knows, you might even make a new friend. Through these types of interactions, we can get the same mindfulness energy as we would through our meditation practice. So, wouldn't it make sense to engage in them more often?

But why wait for someone else to be kind? Why don't we take the initiative and do it ourselves? Smiling and saying a few kind words are easy. Not everyone will respond positively, but that's OK. I think you'll find that most people will. However, if you want to make the greatest connection with other people, there are four things you must do: (1) let your walls down, (2) practice deep listening, (3) cultivate compassion in your heart, and (4) practice forgiveness.

## Letting Your Walls Down

Most of us associate letting our walls down with being vulnerable, but the two aren't necessarily the same. What we're essentially doing when we let our walls down is opening a spiritual connection. More accurately, we are making a conscious contact with another person. We are allowing our consciousness to expand and touch that of others. This is how we exchange our mindfulness energy.

You don't have to tell people your deep dark secrets to open your heart to them. Letting your walls down is essentially a willingness to have a meaningful exchange with someone, and it starts with turning your attention to him and looking into his eyes.

## Practicing Deep Listening

Deep listening will help us connect with other people, especially strangers, at a much deeper level. People know when we're not listening to them and remain reserved, which will diminish our connection with them. Deep listening may be difficult at first because our mind is more agitated, and we're usually preoccupied with our own concerns.

However, as our mind calms down through our meditation practice, we'll get better at it because greater concentration and mindfulness will lead to improved listening skills. You will see for yourself how much people appreciate it when you truly listen to them. I've even had people thank me for listening. It is a win-win situation. We'll talk more about deep listening in Step 8.

## Developing Compassion

Compassion is another useful tool for helping us stay open to other people. We can practice compassion by being mindful of other people's suffering. When people behave in unkind ways, they do so because they are suffering. They are unmindful of how their words and actions affect others. They often blame other people for their misfortunes, so they feel compelled to exact revenge for their suffering.

They may have been abused by family members, or other people who are no longer accessible, so they cannot hold the original transgressor accountable. In such cases, they are often angry with everyone, including themselves, so they treat everyone unkindly because they cannot see beyond their own suffering, and the injustices that were done to them.

It is a challenge to have compassion for people who are abrasive or unkind. Our natural reaction is to shut them out. Eventually, everyone will do something we disapprove of. But if we write off each person after a transgression, then we'll never have any friends. If we want to continue on our path to inner peace, we must learn to see other people's suffering.

## Practicing Forgiveness

Today, I try being open to everyone, no matter how they treat me. It doesn't mean that I'm anyone's doormat. I certainly don't allow people to take advantage of me. It simply means that I don't see the value of getting even with people who may have harmed me. As

> Forgiveness is not about releasing someone from accountability for his actions. It is about us letting go of our anger and resentment.

Gandhi once said, "An eye for an eye only ends up making the whole world blind."

Practicing forgiveness can be a challenge, especially if someone has hurt us, or a loved one. Anger and resentment, whether justified or unjustified, will greatly impede our progress, because they are simply manifestations of the hindrance of aversion.

Forgiveness is not about releasing someone from accountability for his actions. It is about us letting go of our anger and resentment. In order to be forgiving, we must look deeply and see how the transgressor is creating his own suffering. By looking at the situation from a broader perspective, we can transform the mental formations that trigger our anger.

## Learning to Be More Sociable

For some of us, being outgoing and sociable can be difficult. Though we may be born with genetic predispositions regarding our personalities, sociability is generally a learned behavior. Connecting with other people was particularly difficult for me early in my spiritual journey. As a young man, I was so frightened of other people that I had difficulty putting two sentences together during conversations.

My spiritual teacher at the time suggested that I engage in a social activity with friends at least once a week, such as going out for lunch or dinner. Even if I could not afford the meal, I should go and have a glass of water, and spend time getting to know other people. I was terrified, but I did it anyway because I was tired of being a prisoner of myself.

Another suggestion my teacher gave me was to do volunteer work. It could be anything I wanted, so long as it involved working with other people. This helped me in several ways:

- I discovered that I had something to contribute to society.
- It expanded my consciousness beyond my own ego because it got me out of myself.

- I improved my social skills by working with clients and other volunteers.
- It helped me develop self-esteem and self-confidence.
- I made many new friends, and got tremendous joy and fulfillment from the work.

At the time, I didn't understand how or why I benefited from being around other people. I just knew that something was working. I began to feel more a part of the human race. It was a wonderful experience.

> If you want to connect with other people, then you need to be around other people.

As I continued to grow, I came to understand the underlying dynamics of relationships, and the value of connecting with other people to enhance my spiritual development. Volunteering taught me an important lesson: if I want to connect with other people, then I need to be around other people.

It takes some time and effort to develop social skills, but the rewards are tremendous. A complete discussion of this is beyond the scope of this book, but you'll find that as you keep practicing mindfulness meditation, your social skills will develop naturally. If you're interested in a detailed discussion of the subject, I recommend Dale Carnegie's book *How To Win Friends and Influence People*. The practices are just as pertinent today as they were when the book was first published in 1937.

## Wonderful People Are Everywhere!

I'm sure that by now, you're beginning to appreciate the importance of connecting with others to enhance your spiritual development. So then, where can you go to connect with other people? Simply take a look at the places you attend regularly, and go there with an open heart and mind, and you'll see how easy and fun it is to connect with them. It may be a brief encounter, an in-depth conversation, or it may turn into a long-lasting friendship. You may even find a life partner.

You don't necessarily have to engage in a conversation to connect with people. Usually, a smile or a simple greeting will open a connection. Compliments work wonders. Cashiers are especially easy people to connect with, because they're often bored and would welcome a friendly exchange with someone to break up the monotony.

*"Let us always meet each other with a smile, for the smile is the beginning of love."*

~ Mother Teresa

Often a witty comment is enough to bring a smile to someone's face. However, make sure your comment is not demeaning or offensive, because it will backfire. I've learned this lesson the hard way. Here are some of my favorite places to socialize with other people:

**The shopping mall.** The mall is a great place to connect with people because many of them are there for enjoyment or entertainment, such as to buy something for themselves or a loved one. I sometimes take a leisurely stroll (i.e. a mindful walk) and try to make conscious contact with the people there.

**The airport.** The airport can be a stressful place for some of us, but it doesn't have to be. Many people there are vulnerable because they're either being separated or reunited with loved ones, so their hearts are more inclined to be open. Though it may be more difficult to engage them individually, you can make a good connection with many of them at the same time. All you have to do is open your heart and visualize the exchange of mindfulness energy taking place.

**Your church.** Some of you may belong to a church, or another religious organization. At the gatherings, people are usually very warm and friendly. All you have to do is open your heart, and you'll feel the power.

**Twelve-step fellowships.** You may belong to one of the twelve-step fellowships, such as Alcoholics Anonymous or Narcotics Anonymous. Most of the people at the meetings are warm and friendly, and always welcome visitors. There are also other fellowships, such as Al-Anon,

Nar-Anon, and Adult Children of Alcoholics, for anyone whose life has been affected by alcohol or drug use. Most of us would probably qualify for one fellowship or another.

**Your workplace.** This is an excellent place to connect with people. We often take coworkers for granted, since we spend so much time with them, and sometimes treat them as adversaries for various reasons. We sometimes tune them out once we begin to see their flaws and less-than-perfect work ethics. We usually gravitate toward people who see things the same way we do, and ignore the rest.

Most of us work with other people all day long, so why not try connecting with them on a deeper level? With people you don't normally interact with, try looking at them differently. Try talking to them more and practice deep listening. You may find that they're much different than you thought. And if you're fortunate enough to work with the public, then you have many more people with whom to connect.

**Volunteer work.** It's much easier to connect with people when doing volunteer work than in most other situations, because many of them are very open, whether they're on the giving or receiving end. You'll be doing your community a great service by getting involved in a worthy cause, and it will help you make tremendous strides in your spiritual development.

**The post office.** That's right, the post office! Many people see going to the post office as an inconvenience, so it's common for them to be restless and impatient. You can help make it a more pleasant experience for everyone by being cheerful, and saying a few kind words to the clerk, or someone in line. I've found it fairly easy to change the mood there because people are open to someone helping them pass the time.

I once met a gentleman at the post office while standing in line. He was a large humble looking man in his mid-50s. I don't remember what I said to start the conversation, but he began telling me that he had just found a job after being unemployed for about 2 years. At the time, the economy was coming out of a recession, so jobs were hard to come by, especially for someone near retirement age. He was so happy, and I was happy for him.

A few months later, I ran into the same gentleman again at the post office, and I remembered our conversation. I asked him how his new job was going, and he said it was going wonderfully. Our exchange only lasted a total of about five minutes, but it enriched both of our lives. It helps me open my heart each time I think about it.

Other examples of places to connect with people include parks, art festivals, and just about any outdoor event. I'm sure you can probably think of many more. There are some exceptions. You don't want to go where you might be in danger, or there will be a lot of alcohol drinking or use of illicit drugs, because the environment will drain you of your mindfulness energy. Think about the people's frame of mind. You want to go to a place where people are at the very least in a neutral frame of mind. Then you can practice your social skills to try to connect with them.

I would suggest getting involved in an organization where you can attend meetings regularly. The more often you can attend, the better. Meditators who belong to a church or a twelve-step fellowship are able to attend functions several times a week. They're generally the ones who progress the fastest.

I engage other people, including strangers, daily and have a wonderful time with them. The great thing is that we're not only helping ourselves, but we're also helping them. Try it and you'll see for yourself how it enhances your meditation practice: then make it part of your routine. I can assure you that not only will you grow much faster, but you'll also get a tremendous amount of joy and fulfillment out of it.

## The Meditation Group: Your Spiritual Refuge

Now we're going to talk about getting involved in a meditation group, or sangha. For our purposes, I will only talk about starting your own mindfulness meditation group. There are two reasons for this: (1) if there is no sangha in your area that focuses on mindfulness meditation, this will give you some guidance for starting one, and (2) if there is such a sangha near you, then it would be helpful to have a point of reference, so you can determine if it's suitable for your needs.

Starting a sangha is a lot easier than you might think. The challenging part is keeping it focused, because it's tempting to want to try all different kinds of things, and next thing you know, you're no longer practicing mindfulness meditation. As a serious meditator, it's essential to stay grounded in the basics of the practice—developing concentration and mindfulness—if you want to continue making progress.

To make things easy for you, I've prepared a group starter kit that provides you with a sample format, a preamble to help you stay focused, and some literature about the practice. You can download it from the Resources section of our website.

## Starting a Meditation Group Is Easy and Fun

To start a sangha, all you need are two people. Tell your friends and family members about your meditation practice and invite them to join you. What I do is mention it casually in conversation when someone asks me what I've been doing lately. I tell them how I've been meditating and the benefits I've gotten so far, and they're welcome to join me. I've been quite surprised at how many people respond, even people from religious denominations I wouldn't normally expect.

*"The desire to reach for the stars is ambitious. The desire to reach hearts is wise."*

~ MAYA ANGELOU

In fact, the Unitarian Universalist church is quite receptive to meditation groups. It sees meditation as a valuable tool to help its members achieve their spiritual goals. The church here in Raleigh recently asked me to conduct a workshop series for its members.

Oftentimes, meditation is exactly what people are looking for in their lives, especially now that there's such a growing interest in mindfulness meditation. So think of all the people you'd be helping by showing them how to meditate. We'll talk more in-depth about sangha-building in Step 12. I'll give you some suggestions on how to keep members involved, not only in the sangha, but also in their own practice.

## Where to Meet

Once you have a small group, you will need a place to meet. You can start by meeting at one of the member's house, and as your sangha grows, you can easily find another place. There are many churches that rent out rooms, and their fees are often minimal.

If you find a facility that is free, I strongly recommend that you insist on paying something. You should always strive to remain self-supporting. This will ensure that you remain autonomous, and don't have to answer to any outside organizations. You can fund your group by passing a basket during your meeting and asking members to make a small contribution. Usually, a dollar or two per member per session will be enough to pay your expenses.

## When to Meet

Next, you need to decide when to meet. Keep in mind that you'll never find a time that's convenient for everyone. Many groups meet on a weekday in the early evening starting somewhere between 6 p.m. and 8 p.m. for 1-1½ hours. This time works well for people who work during the day because it gives them a chance to go home, have dinner, and then go to the meeting.

Other groups prefer to meet on the weekend early in the day, which allows for other activities the rest of the day. Sunday evening often works well for some people. Some groups even meet early in the morning, such as 6 or 7 a.m. I don't know how they do that, but it works for them. These are just some ideas, but ultimately, you have to pick a time that is most suitable for your members.

One more thing about when to meet: nothing says that you have to meet only once a week. In fact, the more often you meet, the better. Why do you think monks and nuns progress so quickly? It's because they usually meditate with their sangha every day, in addition to meditating alone.

> How much you progress in your spiritual development is directly proportional to the effort you put into your practice.

Now, I'm not suggesting that you have to take it that far, but always remember this: how much you progress in your spiritual development is directly proportional to the effort you put into your practice. It is up to you to find a balance between your meditation practice and your commitments.

## Staying Focused on Your Primary Purpose

Lack of focus on mindfulness meditation will greatly diminish the effectiveness of your sangha. Once a group loses its focus, it's just about impossible to get it back, because members will become accustomed to the loose format. I've seen this happen many times. To help you stay focused on your primary purpose—to learn and practice mindfulness meditation—I recommend having a preamble, which includes your guiding principles. The groups I've seen stay focused are the ones that read their preamble at the beginning of every meeting.

Now, this doesn't mean that you become rigid and inflexible. On the contrary, with the mindfulness meditation practice, there is plenty of room for variety and creativity. The whole idea behind staying focused is to stay grounded in the basics of the practice, and to keep moving forward. If your message isn't clear, then newcomers will be confused about your purpose, and will have difficulty seeing the benefit of participating in your group. They may attend a few sessions, but will soon lose interest, especially if they're not learning how to meditate.

Once you have some guiding principles, you can think about the level of practice you want to focus on, that is, beginning or intermediate level. Advanced level is beyond most of us, so I won't discuss it now. Choosing the best level of practice to focus on in your meetings can be a challenge, because everyone is at a different level. If your meetings are geared toward the intermediate level, then newcomers will be lost and won't return. If seasoned members always have to practice beginning level, their progress will stagnate.

So, what can you do? When your sangha starts out, I suggest a beginning level format so that everyone has a chance to learn the basics of the practice. Once your members gain some experience, you can have two meetings—one for beginners, and the other for experienced members. You may want to schedule them back to back, because some members will want to attend both. You may come up with a more creative solution to this dilemma, but remember that you always want newcomers to feel welcome by addressing their need for basic instruction.

The main thing to keep in mind is that you want to both teach and practice mindfulness meditation, so always include some form of instruction along with at least thirty minutes of meditation. This will enable your members to experience the power of the mindfulness meditation practice.

## Conclusion

In Step 7, you learned about the value of meditating with other people, and the basics of starting your own sangha. You also learned how to achieve the greatest spiritual connections in your interactions and relationships with others.

Meditating and connecting with other people are important elements of your mindfulness meditation practice, because without them you'll deprive yourself of the sources of mindfulness energy vital to your spiritual and emotional development. They will also make your life more enjoyable and fulfilling, because you will learn how to cultivate more meaningful relationships.

In the next step, I'll show you how to use deep listening and mindful speech to enhance your spiritual connections with others. You'll find out just how powerful these tools are for healing and transforming your relationships. In Step 12, we'll discuss sangha-building more in-depth, and I'll show you how it can take your spiritual development to an even higher level.

If you're shy, like I was, you know that life can feel like a prison. It can be a lonely and painful existence. The good news is that you don't have to feel that way. If you follow the suggestions I've outlined in this step, you'll soon have some truly wonderful relationships in your life, and you'll no longer be a prisoner of yourself. I realize that it can be scary at first, but I'm confident that the practice will help you overcome your fears.

## Exercises

The following exercises are designed to help you connect with other people on a deeper level, and tap into the unlimited source of mindfulness energy that is freely available. I'm sure you'll find them easy to put into practice, and you'll get tremendous enjoyment and fulfillment from them.

**1. Practice opening up to others.** When you're around other people, practice being warm, friendly, and open, instead of ignoring them and getting lost in your own thoughts. Try smiling and making eye contact. Not everyone will respond positively, but most will. Chances are that many people need a friendly smile from someone. It's easy and rewarding to help someone who's having a rough day.

**2. Spend time around other people.** Go some place where there are many people you don't know, and try tuning into their spiritual presence. Some examples are: a shopping mall, an airport, a church, a twelve-step meeting, or the grocery store. Just about any church will work great. You don't necessarily have to accept their doctrine, or become a member. What you're looking for is an environment where people are open and friendly, so you can connect and share mindfulness energy with them. I suggest doing this exercise regularly, such as once or twice a month. With some practice, this openness with other people will become the norm.

**3.  Get involved in a mindfulness meditation group (a sangha).** If one is not available near you, then start your own. It is vital to your development to have the support of other meditators. All you need is one other person to start a sangha. When talking to other people, mention that you've started meditating, and if they seem interested, let them know that you're looking for other people to meditate with. Remember, you'll be helping them too.

Another option is to contact your local Unitarian Universalist church and let them know that you would be interested in starting a meditation group there, and that it would be open to its members. They will likely be receptive to the idea. Keep in mind that you want your meditation group to remain a separate entity from the church, and any other organization. Otherwise, you will lose control of your group.

If you need help getting started, remember that our website has a variety of resources, including a free group starter kit. It contains a preamble, sample format, and literature you can distribute freely.

# STEP 8

## Powerful Tools to Transform and Deepen Your Relationships

*When we are motivated by compassion and wisdom, the results of our actions benefit everyone, not just our individual selves or some immediate convenience.*

~ Dalai Lama

### Chapter Highlights

- Transform Your Relationships with Deep Listening
- Cultivate Peace and Harmony with Mindful Speech
- Develop True Compassion through Non-judging and Forgiveness
- Conclusion
- Exercises

**Step 8**   *"We sought to cultivate peace and harmony in our rela-*
*tionships and interactions with others by practicing deep*
*listening, mindful speech, non-judging, and forgiveness."*

EVEN AFTER YEARS OF PRACTICE, I am still amazed at how effective
mindfulness meditation is in transforming people's lives. Occasionally, students come up to me all excited about the dramatic changes
they've seen in themselves after implementing the techniques I've
taught them. They are enthusiastic and want to learn more.

Many of us begin a meditation practice without much thought about
what we can do to improve its effectiveness. Some people believe that
all there is to a meditation practice is to simply sit still for a few minutes
observing their breath. This belief is common even among experienced
meditators. While this approach will certainly yield some results, it is
just the beginning. There are many ways of getting more from your
efforts—much more.

The problem is that many people do not fully understand meditation,
and therefore, are not sure how to improve their practice. If this applies
to you, then you're missing out on a valuable opportunity—the opportunity to overcome your suffering and achieve inner peace much quicker.

In Step 8, you're going to learn how to practice deep listening,
mindful speech, non-judging, and forgiveness. These are tools you can
put into practice immediately. Not only will they enhance your practice,
but they will also improve your relationships with loved ones, friends,
and associates. They will even improve your interactions with strangers.
As you remember from Step 7, strangers can also be valuable sources of
spiritual nourishment.

## Transform Your Relationships with Deep Listening

Deep listening is a helpful tool for developing concentration and
mindfulness. Think of a time when you were engaged in a conversation

with someone, and the other person listened to you with great interest. How did it make you feel? Did you feel a connection with the person? Did you feel uplifted or energized? I certainly feel these things when someone is listening to me, or when I'm the one doing the listening. There are two reasons for this: (1) we are making a spiritual connection with another person, and (2) it brings us into the present moment, which is where reality and mindfulness energy exist.

One of the reasons we have difficulty listening is because we're usually preoccupied with coming up with a response. We are more concerned with getting our point across, than we are in listening to someone else's opinion. This is especially the case when we're engaged in a power struggle. It is more important for us to win the argument, than to achieve greater understanding.

Deep listening is an application of concentration and mindfulness in conversation. As these skills improve through our meditation practice, so will our ability to listen. This is why it is essential to develop them.

Practicing deep listening is not very complicated. The hard part is remembering to do it. The first thing we need to do is refrain from talking. We cannot listen if we're busy talking. Very often, we're so concerned about being heard that we feel compelled to talk nonstop. Furthermore, if our mind is agitated, silence can be quite uncomfortable.

> *"Most people do not listen with the intent to understand; they listen with the intent to reply."*
>
> ~ STEPHEN R. COVEY

When we allow other people to speak and listen to them, they'll be more inclined to listen to us when they're finished. Deep listening conveys a sense of trust and respect. You let the other person know that you respect his opinion, regardless of whether or not you agree with it.

Next, we must pay attention to people with whom we're engaged, and not be distracted by things going on around us, or in our mind. Look into their eyes and pay close attention to what they're saying. If we're distracted, they will know and we won't make a connection. Our distractions will come in the form of one of the Five Hindrances. When they arise, simply acknowledge their presence, and then return to listening.

If you are momentarily distracted and miss something important, the best thing to do is simply admit it, and ask people to repeat what they just said. There's nothing wrong with admitting you were distracted. In fact, this is a clear indication that you're truly interested in what they're saying, and they'll be happy to repeat it. They will also appreciate your sincerity.

> Deep listening can bring about a tremendous amount of healing to a wounded heart, especially that of a young child.

Deep listening can bring about a tremendous amount of healing to a wounded heart, especially that of a young child. Children are usually open and receptive. It gives them the spiritual nurturing vital to their emotional development. Sometimes when we're busy, we don't have time to listen to our children, and the message they receive is that they're not important. If we do this too often, they will stop confiding in us when they have a problem. Try deep listening with your children. I think you'll be amazed at the results.

I once knew a young girl who always spoke in short bursts. She developed this habit from her interactions with her parents. They rarely allowed her to express herself, so whenever she wanted to say something to them, she had to say it quickly before her parents had the chance to interrupt her.

One day, her parents came to me exasperated because their daughter was unruly and would not follow direction, and asked me if I could help. The next day, I spent the afternoon with their daughter, and her sister, with whom they were having similar difficulties. I took them to a nearby park where we practiced walking meditation for a while. Afterward, we sat on the grass, and I just let them talk. They told me all kinds of things; personal things they could not tell their parents.

On the way back home, we stopped for pizza, and they continued talking. The next day, their mother called me up and asked me what I had said to their daughters. I asked, "What do you mean?" She said,

"Well, they're completely different. They're no longer giving us a hard time. What did you say to them?" I thought about it for a couple of seconds and then replied, "I didn't say anything. I just listened to them."

As parents, it's important to be mindful of our children's changing needs. When they're infants, they don't have the capability of protecting themselves from harm and providing for their own needs, so they are completely dependent on us for their survival. In addition, we are their primary source of spiritual nourishment.

As they become teenagers, their needs change significantly. They are now more mentally and emotionally developed, and have a greater need for independence. They need the freedom to make some decisions that affect their lives. They also have a need to connect with other sources of spiritual nourishment—their peers.

Some parents do not recognize these changing needs, so they continue treating their teenagers as infants that are still fully dependent on them, and unable to make decisions for themselves. This is usually a source of conflict between teenagers and their parents.

A more mindful way to address such a situation would be to acknowledge our teenagers' needs for independence. Then help them make this transition by teaching them how to have healthy relationships with other people, and give them increasing responsibilities, with consequences associated with those responsibilities. This way, they can learn from their mistakes, and gain valuable life experience.

Deep listening is an effective tool for dealing with our growing children. It sends them a clear message that what they have to say is important, at a time when they need to hear it the most. Remember, the energy of mindfulness can heal and transform not just ourselves, but others as well. Deep listening can improve your relationships with loved ones, because it gives them the spiritual nourishment they need to grow. You also let them know that they're important to you. They will see that you appreciate them, and they'll begin to appreciate you in return.

## Cultivate Peace and Harmony with Mindful Speech

Mindful speech is another useful tool that can heal and transform our lives. When used properly, it can bring much peace and harmony in all our interactions with people. It is similar to deep listening in that it is also an application of concentration and mindfulness. Mindful speech is not too difficult to learn. The results are immediate, and it will have a significant impact on our relationships. Mindful speech can help us in various ways:

- **Improves our connections with other people.** By choosing words that are more loving and respectful, we can put other people at ease and allow them to open their heart and share their mindfulness energy with us. This will help us both grow spiritually. It's a win-win situation.

- **Helps loved ones overcome their pain and suffering.** We can help other people heal the wounds in their heart. Kind words let them know that we truly care about them. Mindful speech is particularly healing for young children.

- **Helps us live in the present moment.** Whenever we're mindful of our actions, we come back to the present moment. This will enable us to dwell in our True Nature—the source of mindfulness energy within us.

- **Improves our performance at work, or at school.** By choosing our words carefully, we reduce conflicts and misunderstandings. This will make us more effective leaders.

We can also take mindful speech to a higher level, so we can be more effective in helping others transform their lives. As you grow spiritually, you will develop the wisdom necessary to be of maximum service to society.

My first big lesson on mindful speech came on my first of several retreats with Zen master Thich Nhat Hanh, or Thay as we called him. I arrived early in the evening just as the retreat was starting, while he was giving an orientation talk and the guidelines for the retreat. I was a little flustered because I was trying to check in quickly at the registration desk, so I could get to the orientation. To make matters worse, there was a problem with my room assignment, which I would have to deal with afterwards.

Once I got to the orientation, I relaxed a little; but since it was my first retreat, I was still rather apprehensive. I went there by myself without knowing anyone, but I was still looking forward to an interesting experience. When Thay was almost finished, he told us that we were going to practice noble silence for the next four days, beginning immediately. During this time, we were to refrain from speaking altogether. If we truly needed to communicate with someone, we could use the notepads we received in our registration packet.

A wave of panic came over me. I thought, "How am I going to get by, and how am I going to resolve the issue with my room?" After a few minutes, I began to wonder what the big deal was. So what if I can't speak for a few days? It's not going to kill me. After all, I could use the notepad to communicate if I needed. Well, for the next four days, whenever I needed to communicate something with the notepad, I thought carefully about what I really needed to say and how I could say it concisely, since I had to write it out by hand.

The other interesting thing I noticed was that I felt rather defenseless without the ability to speak, and I began to wonder why. I slowly realized that I used my speech to manipulate other people into doing or giving me what I wanted. What's more, the manipulation was very subtle. Since then, I've been a lot more careful about what I say to people. I am more mindful of my motives for saying something, and how I say it. I've found that sometimes it's best to say nothing, and just listen.

> We should choose words that are kind, loving, and healing.

Many people pride themselves in telling it like it is. This is actually a misnomer. Unless we are truly enlightened, none of us fully understand the nature of any situation. So what they are really doing is telling it the way they see it, that is, their view or opinion, which is probably not entirely accurate. Usually, the motive behind doing this is to throw people off balance, and make them unsure of themselves by being critical. When they succeed, they get a boost of energy at the expense of their victim. It robs the other person of his mindfulness energy. This is not mindful speech.

Whatever the motives behind our speech, we must practice mindfulness when interacting with others if we want to cultivate peace and harmony. We should choose words that are kind, loving, and healing. Now, this doesn't necessarily mean that we have to agree with people just to keep the peace. We can engage in a constructive debate in order to achieve greater understanding, and we can do this in a respectful manner, without provoking anger and resentment in other people.

Sometimes, we want to get even with someone for hurting us. Other times, we just want to get the upper hand in a situation or relationship, so we engage in a power struggle to get people to accept our point of view. Before we speak, we should ask ourselves if what we're about to say will improve a situation, or make it worse.

There may also be times when we need to be assertive. In such cases, we can do so without being unnecessarily provocative. Whatever the case, I think that if we examine our motives, we'll find that much of our speech is unnecessary. Remember, no speech is usually better than unmindful speech.

I think the best way to learn how to practice mindful speech is the way I learned—through a retreat that incorporates noble silence. This will force us to examine the motives behind our speech, and help us choose our words more carefully.

Another method I find effective is to pause before I say something, and resist the temptation to simply react to what someone says. It isn't always necessary for me to give my opinion. In fact, I've found that the less I speak, the more inclined people will be to listen to me when I do speak. And if I choose my words carefully, they can have a much greater impact.

In time, you will develop mindful speech naturally as the result of your meditation practice. As you develop inner peace, your words will become more loving, gentle, and healing.

## Develop True Compassion through Non-judging and Forgiveness

Now we're going to look at a behavior that gets in the way of our spiritual development. This is our condemnation of other people. It is an obstacle because when people do things we disapprove of, our natural reaction is to put up a wall and disconnect from them spiritually, which prevents the free flow of mindfulness energy. We also diminish the connection with our True Nature, which further restricts the flow of mindfulness energy. This is a situation where everyone involved loses.

There are two factors at work when we condemn other people:

- **Attachment to our views.** When other people do things differently, we often assume they're wrong, and we're right.

- **The hindrance of aversion.** We often try to avoid unpleasant situations, or we try to change them to meet our approval.

We all judge people to some degree. We use our judgment to assess whether or not someone is trustworthy. We generally expect others to act civilized and use good judgment. So what is our reaction when they don't? It depends mainly on three things:

- **The severity of the transgression.** Did someone make an unkind remark, or commit a serious crime? Of course, the more serious the transgression, the more harshly we judge people.

- **If the transgression was directed at us, or a loved one.** We generally try to protect people we care about the most, such as our family, friends, and ourselves. We also try to protect places and things with which we have some form of affiliation, such as our home, community, or country.

- **Our emotional sensitivity.** Emotional sensitivity is simply a concern for our own feelings. For example, someone may say something that hurts our feelings. Emotional sensitivity is rooted in the ego. In fact, all emotions are rooted in the ego, because they are our reactions based on our views about the world. This form of sensitivity is not compassion, which is more of a genuine concern for others' well-being.

Many of us can accept other people's fallibility, but it may be more difficult if someone commits a serious injustice. Keep in mind that excusing and accepting people's actions are two entirely different things. By excusing, we're justifying their behavior. By accepting, we're forgiving them, regardless of whether their behavior was right or wrong. We can accept someone's transgression without excusing it.

How we react to an injustice will vary, but generally, we tend to put up a wall either temporarily or permanently. The biggest problem is when we put up a permanent wall toward people, in the form of resentment. If we are very sensitive, we'll write them off permanently. Now, considering that we're all fallible, and eventually we're all going to do something to hurt someone else, what do you think will happen when we write off each person who hurts us? We're going to end up alone, with no friends or family in our lives.

> *"How people treat you is their karma; how you react is yours."*
>
> ~ WAYNE W. DYER

This usually happens when we have unrealistic expectations of other people. Eventually, they will fall short, and if we have difficulty accepting that, the only ones we'll be able to get along with will be our pets. They love us unconditionally because they can't see our faults. They don't have the capability of being judgmental. If only we could learn to practice unconditional love that way with other people, then we would have the same kind of loving relationships with them.

There are two good indicators of when we are being judgmental. The first is when we start feeling annoyed. When we're annoyed at someone or a situation, it means that somebody did something that didn't meet our expectations or standards. When this happens, we immediately begin shutting down our spiritual connection with the individuals involved.

The second indicator is when we express our disapproval through complaining. This is our annoyance taken a step further. We often complain to seek validation: we want justification for our anger. Sometimes we complain to make a connection with people, that is, to get their attention and agreement with our point of view. The problem is that the mindfulness energy we derive from this is limited. So to keep the energy flowing, we need to keep complaining. However, this doesn't work with everyone. Most people don't like to hear constant complaining. Do you?

> *"An eye for an eye only ends up making the whole world blind."*
>
> ~ MAHATMA GANDHI

It is surprisingly simple to overcome unwholesome judgment of other people. To a great extent, it will happen naturally through your meditation practice. What will probably have the most immediate and profound impact is writing meditation, which we'll discuss in Step 9. Through these practices, the following five elements will come together to dramatically change the way you see and feel about other people:

- **Willingness.** Nothing will change unless we're willing to make a sincere and diligent effort to change. The fact that you're reading this book demonstrates that you have the willingness.

- **Mindfulness.** As your mindfulness develops through your meditation practice, you will gain more clarity and wisdom, and see how your behavior is affecting you and those around you.

- **Compassion.** People don't treat others unkindly if they are happy, joyous, and free. They do it because they are not at peace. If we can see other people's suffering, we may not judge them so harshly. Maybe they're dealing with an illness in their family, or they have many painful memories that they have not yet overcome.

- **Forgiveness.** Once we have judged someone harshly, we become either angry or resentful. As we develop compassion, it will become easier to let go of our anger and resentment.

- **Mindfulness energy.** As we cultivate the energy of mindfulness through our practice, we will become stronger spiritually. Then we'll become more mindful, compassionate, and forgiving. We will no longer be so attached to our views, and anger and resentment will just melt away, making it easier to practice unconditional love with everyone.

## Conclusion

In this step, you learned how to practice deep listening, mindful speech, non-judging, and forgiveness. These are valuable tools that will not only enhance your meditation practice, but will also make your relationships and interactions with other people much more enjoyable. They will truly enrich your life. Furthermore, they will help you achieve inner peace much faster.

> When you see for yourself that we are all interconnected, loneliness and insecurity will simply disappear.

In the next step, you will learn about some even more powerful tools you can apply to your practice. I believe that once you apply these tools, you will reach a point in your spiritual development where the practice will become a way of life for you. You will then reach a level of mental and emotional maturity that you never thought possible.

As you progress in your practice, you will gain a deeper appreciation of the full power of the mindfulness meditation practice. You will become more peaceful and confident as you find your place in the world, and your whole life will begin to make complete sense. And when you see for yourself that we are all interconnected, loneliness and insecurity will simply disappear.

## Exercises

The following exercises will help you develop mindfulness when interacting with other people. You will be amazed at how your relationships will improve simply by practicing deep listening and mindful speech. People will find you more enjoyable and pleasant to be around.

**1. Practice deep listening.** Begin applying concentration and mindfulness to your conversations with other people. Look into their eyes and truly listen to what they are saying. Avoid looking around to see everything else going on in the room, and put aside any distracting thoughts.

You can ask follow-up questions to help keep your attention focused. This will signal to them that you're really listening. Observe how their behavior changes as a result of your listening. The first few times you practice deep listening, write down your observations in your meditation journal.

**2. Practice mindful speech.** Resist the temptation to always give your opinion on matters. When you do find it necessary to speak, examine your motives and choose your words carefully, so that they create peace and harmony, and not ill will. Choose words that are loving, kind, and healing. Help the other person feel at ease around you.

The first few times you practice mindful speech, write down your observations in your meditation journal, and think about how you can improve your handling of similar situations in the future.

**3. Practice non-judging and forgiveness.** Observe your reaction when someone does something you don't like, or disagree with. Notice the words that come out of your mouth. Are they kind, or unkind words? Do you then look for someone else to agree with you? This should raise a red flag.

Try looking deeper into other people's motives for their behavior, and cultivate compassion for their suffering. If you have already become angry with someone, stop feeding it. Stop trying to justify your anger: then let it go, and try forgiving the person. Remember, you don't have to excuse people's behavior to forgive them. The first few times you practice non-judging and forgiveness, write down your observations in your meditation journal.

# STEP 9

## How to Make Mindfulness a Way of Life

*The few cross over to the far shore. The many merely run back and forth fruitlessly along the side of the stream.*

~ BUDDHA

### Chapter Highlights

- The Present Moment: Your Gateway to Enlightenment
- Finding the Present Moment through Mindful Living
- Unconditional Love through Loving-Kindness Meditation
- Writing Meditation: Your Second Most Powerful Tool
- The Mindfulness Meditation Retreat: Your Most Powerful Tool
- Conclusion
- Exercises

**Step 9**   *"We sought to dwell deeply in our spiritual community in order to enhance our development, and that of others."*

I'VE HAD PEOPLE TELL ME that they're not interested in becoming a guru: they just want to learn how to be happy. While this sentiment may sound humble, and noble, it is not practical. You see, true happiness comes only with wisdom, and not material possessions or outside circumstances. It is only when we have a much greater understanding of the consequences of our thoughts and actions that we can behave in more loving and harmonious ways. True happiness and wisdom are inseparable.

You've probably met people who seem to be happy, who are kind and compassionate, and always involved in giving back to society, while others are more preoccupied with their own lives. Chances are that these people have learned how to live in the present moment. They have accepted their past, and are not worried about the future. They have seen their interconnectedness with the rest of humanity, so they realize their welfare is tied to the welfare of others.

*"Happiness does not come from consumption of things."*

~ THICH NHAT HANH

The problem that many people have is their misconception of what leads to happiness. They usually point to their successful career, family, and material possessions as evidence of their happiness. But as you've probably realized by now, all these things are impermanent and bring only temporary pleasure. When they lose these things, they will also lose their happiness.

We can't achieve true happiness until we understand our suffering and learn how to eliminate it. As long as our happiness depends on things that are impermanent, we will always be disappointed. Furthermore, as long as our practice remains only a part of our lives, our spiritual growth and freedom from suffering will be limited.

If we want to achieve long-lasting peace and serenity, then our spiritual practice must become a way of life, and our happiness must depend on something that is constant. One thing in our lives that is constant is the present moment, and this is at the core of mindful living.

In Step 9, you're going to learn how to make mindfulness a way of life, instead of just a part of your life. But in order to fully appreciate the importance of this commitment, you need to experience the full power of the mindfulness meditation practice.

In this step, you will learn about mindful living, writing meditation, and the mindfulness meditation retreat. These are the most powerful tools in your meditation practice. They will help you take your spiritual, mental, and emotional development to a higher level—a road traveled by the few who are truly determined to make a significant positive impact in the world.

## The Present Moment: Your Gateway to Enlightenment

I've already shown you how to incorporate mindful breathing and mindful walking into your practice, but I have not yet fully explained why these two activities are so important. What makes them useful tools for enhancing our practice is that they keep us grounded in the present moment. Let's look at this more in-depth.

> Mindful breathing and mindful walking keep us grounded in the present moment.

We're all familiar with the concept of time. We generally think of it as a series of moments passing by at the same rate, and we measure it in equal size increments, such as seconds, minutes, hours, days, and so on. For all practical purposes, this concept works pretty well for most of our activities. However, it is not entirely accurate.

Time does not pass at the same rate everywhere. This isn't something that I or anyone else has made up. Albert Einstein demonstrated this through his theory of relativity, and it's generally accepted among physicists and other scientists.

Einstein showed that time passes at different rates according to how fast an object is traveling. The faster it travels; the slower time will pass for the object. To demonstrate this phenomenon, scientists use two very accurate clocks. They put one on a spacecraft that orbits the earth, and keep the other one on the ground. The idea is that the clock traveling at several thousand miles per hour will experience the passage of time differently than the stationary clock. When the spacecraft returns to earth, they compare them, and each time, the clocks show a difference, just as predicted.

So, what does all this have to do with our everyday lives? Well, one example is the performance of the navigation equipment in our automobile. It uses a global positioning system (GPS) for tracking the location of our vehicle relative to other objects on the ground, and they tell us how far our destination is from our location. The satellite tracking these positions is orbiting the earth at very high speeds, and it has to take into account the difference in the passage of time, or it will give us inaccurate directions.

The whole point of this discussion about time is that if we're going to see the true nature of reality, we should be aware that time doesn't always pass at the same rate everywhere. This opens the door to many possibilities with regards to the nature of our existence.

We often talk about living deeply in the present moment. There is an important reason for this. Actually, there are various reasons. From a practical standpoint, the present moment is where the human experience is always taking place. The past is already gone, and the future will always remain in the future.

Our experience is in the here and now, and nowhere else. When we get all caught up in thinking about the past and the future, we are not being fully engaged in what is taking place where we actually are. In other words, we are not in touch with reality.

At a deeper level, the present moment is where a whole other reality exists. It is where our True Nature resides, and if we want it to shine through, then we must dwell deeply the present moment. The present moment is similar to our True Nature in the sense that it has no dimensions of time or space.

Scientists have been unable to identify a physical component of consciousness. Sure, they might be able to describe it in terms of electrical impulses that make up thought patterns, but where are the images projected? We know the images exist because we can see them in our mind, but they have no physical dimensions, which is a requirement for something to exist in the physical universe.

Scientists have had difficulty studying consciousness because they've been unable to measure it. This is why they've left the study of consciousness to religious thinkers and philosophers, who use different methods.

In the mindfulness meditation practice, we investigate the nature of reality by observing it. Instead of developing a theory and trying to prove it to the rest of the world, we learn to see reality for ourselves, and then we teach others how to see it for themselves. This is why it's so important to develop our observation skills. Using this approach, not only will we begin to understand reality, but we will also transform our lives in the process.

> All it takes is touching one moment very deeply, and the full force of mindfulness energy comes flooding through like a tidal wave of peace and serenity.

By observing with clarity, we can simply look at a phenomenon and understand its nature. As we awaken our True Nature, we awaken another sense for perceiving the world. In addition, we will see a world that doesn't exist within the confines of time and space. It is the world of consciousness, and it exists deeply in the present moment.

If you've ever had a profound spiritual experience, then you've touched the present moment very deeply. It feels like time comes to a complete stop, and you're in a reality outside the space-time continuum. There is no pain and suffering there—only peace, tranquility, and vast knowledge. It is where we find the unlimited source of mindfulness energy. The Buddhists call this nirvana.

This is why we place so much emphasis on living in the present moment. All it takes is touching one moment very deeply, and the full force of mindfulness energy comes flooding through like a tidal wave of peace and serenity.

So how do you touch nirvana? You do it by training yourself to be in the present moment. Your awakening can come quickly, or it can come slowly. It all depends on how much right effort you put into your practice. If you keep practicing mindfulness meditation and living mindfully, you will gradually immerse yourself in the vast ocean of mindfulness energy. And if conditions are sufficient, you will suddenly get pulled in without warning. It is a wonderful experience when this happens.

## Finding the Present Moment through Mindful Living

Practicing mindfulness in our daily activities can be quite a challenge, if we don't have the proper tools. Many of our activities become so routine that we can do them without thinking. Then we begin occupying our mind with other things we think are productive. But are they really?

Sometimes our mind drifts off thinking about the past or the future, or we simply worry about things. This usually happens when we're engaged in a routine activity we consider boring. Remember, we generally want to avoid pain, and for some of us, boredom can be quite uncomfortable. So to avoid boredom, we engage in fantasies to stimulate sensual pleasure. This certainly isn't productive, at least not for our spiritual development.

Routine activities are great opportunities to practice concentration and mindfulness. They will help you stay grounded in the present moment. We can take a routine activity, such as washing dishes, and turn it into a meditation session. The only difference is the object of our meditation. Simply apply the techniques that I've shown you for sitting meditation. The results will be the same. In fact, you may find yourself looking deeply into one of the dishes, and notice it glowing. So pick some routine activities, and turn them into meditation sessions. Whether they be ironing, folding clothes, mowing the lawn, or taking out the trash, they are all wonderful opportunities to further your spiritual development.

When performing one of these activities, make a diligent effort to practice concentration or mindfulness, and keep bringing yourself back whenever you drift away in thought. This may sound boring, but it's not. As you gain a deeper awareness of the present moment, you'll begin to access the source of mindfulness energy within you, and the world will truly come alive.

There may be more complex activities that require greater attention, such as work-related tasks, or cooking a meal. The next time you engage in these activities, see if you can apply your mindfulness skills to improve your performance.

As you can see, concentration and mindfulness have applications to all our daily activities. You can either use them to aid your spiritual development, or to perform those activities in a more efficient and effective manner. Either way, they will enrich your life.

Incorporating concentration and mindfulness into our activities is not very difficult. The hard part is remembering to do it. It's easy to get lost in our thoughts whenever we don't need to use our mind to perform a task. It may be helpful in the beginning to post a few notes in strategic places at home or at work, to remind you to be more mindful. In time, mindfulness will come to you naturally.

## Unconditional Love through Loving-Kindness Meditation

Loving-kindness is the ideal form of love. It is unconditional love, meaning that it extends to all people, regardless of whether or not they deserve it. There are also no expectations of receiving anything in return—only giving. With loving-kindness, we share love with everyone we encounter simply because we care about all living beings.

Sometimes, our love for other people depends on how they behave. We often place conditions on our love without even knowing it. A clear indication of when our love has conditions is when we feel unappreciated. We obviously want some recognition or reciprocation for our good deeds, and we feel disappointed when we don't get it.

Our society places great emphasis on showing appreciation to our loved ones, especially in intimate relationships. In Western society, couples are taught to expect appreciation from their partner. In Buddhist psychology, it's considered wholesome to show appreciation, but not to expect to receive it. Those who give unconditionally are just as content whether or not anyone appreciates their kindness. Expressing appreciation does have some healing effects for the recipient, but by continuing to expect it from loved ones, we prevent ourselves from learning to love unconditionally.

Our love can also depend on whether or not someone's behavior is just. We all have certain concepts of justice. We've come to believe that people deserve to be either rewarded or punished for their deeds. This belief is so deeply ingrained in most societies that we have judicial systems to determine guilt or innocence for violations of our laws, and to dispense punishment accordingly. There is nothing inherently wrong with this. We certainly don't want dangerous people free to commit violent crimes as they wish. Law and order is necessary to prevent societies from slipping into anarchy.

The problem lies in our own mind. When someone does something unjust, we usually become angry, and we may feel completely justified in our anger. However, that anger is mostly hurting us because it's keeping us from growing spiritually.

Remember that one of the main qualities of our True Nature is pure love, or unconditional love. If our love for other people depends on some condition, such as good behavior, then it keeps our mind closed and prevents us from accessing the sources of mindfulness energy. So by practicing loving-kindness, we're opening our heart to all people and living beings, regardless of whether their actions are just, or unjust. It will help us see their suffering, so that we can develop compassion for them.

True unconditional love can be a challenge to practice in the beginning. The good news is that you can develop it quickly through loving-kindness meditation. The whole purpose of this practice is to transform our attitudes about other people and living beings, so that we can open ourselves to the rich sources of mindfulness energy available to us all.

There are several physical and psychological benefits of loving-kindness meditation. One study at Stanford University showed that as little as seven minutes each day of loving-kindness meditation increased social connectedness. That is, we feel more connected with the rest of humanity and are more inclined to engage other people in conversation and activities. Another study showed that it reduces pain, anger, and psychological distress in patients with lower back pain.

Loving-kindness meditation is a common practice in Buddhism. It was originally taught by the Buddha himself and has remained an essential part of various Buddhist traditions, including Theravada. Traditionally, loving-kindness meditation has involved either visualizing, reciting, reading, or listening to a set of affirmations, but we've found a different way.

## Writing Meditation: Your Second Most Powerful Tool

While the traditional loving-kindness meditation practice has some effect, here at the Mindfulness Meditation Institute we've developed a different approach. We call it writing meditation. It is a simple, yet extremely effective, way of modifying our behavior in a short period of time. I've seen people completely change their demeanor in just a matter of a week or two. They've become more compassionate, understanding, and forgiving of other people. They've also become more committed to their meditation practice, and they've overcome stubborn habits they've had their entire lives.

What's so amazing about writing meditation is that these changes take place without any conscious effort, and the exercise takes only about ten minutes per day. It's quite effective in helping cultivate a more harmonious environment in group settings, such as the workplace or classroom. Group members begin to see the broader implications of their actions. It works best when all participants do the exercise.

Writing meditation is an accelerated learning technique. What it does is reprogram our subconscious in a way that seems to be much more effective than simply reading, hearing, or reciting the loving-kindness affirmations.

The way we developed writing meditation was almost accidental. One day, as I was writing one of the chapters for this book, I asked a friend to try an exercise that I was thinking of including. The exercise was simple: in a notebook, copy by hand the loving-kindness meditation for about 10-15 minutes every day. I also did the exercise, so we could compare notes after a couple of weeks. I was pretty certain that it would have some positive effect, but I didn't realize how much.

About four days later, my friend came to me all excited about the exercise. She said that it had completely changed her way of thinking. She was being more understanding, compassionate, and loving toward other people. I also noticed a big difference in her. She was becoming more outgoing and sociable, where she had been rather shy and inhibited her whole life. She was becoming the person exemplified in the loving-kindness meditation. The most amazing part was that all of it happened naturally, whereas before she had to remind herself to be kind and loving to other people.

My friend also began sleeping much better. Before the writing exercise, getting a good night's sleep was hit and miss. After she began the exercise, she slept well almost every night. I also experienced better sleep.

I was truly astounded. I never thought the exercise would so easily change someone's entire personality in just a matter of days. I saw similar changes in myself, though not as dramatic because I was already living the principles of the meditation to some extent, though it had taken me years to progress this far. What the exercise did for me was made practicing mindfulness much easier and more natural. I also felt more focused and committed to the practice.

As I thought about why the exercise was so effective, I realized that it was essentially reprogramming our subconscious mind. By writing the meditation, we were imprinting those principles in our mind, so that they changed our views about the world and other people. Once they were imprinted in our subconscious, they began manifesting themselves in our conscious mind, and then in our actions. Also, the daily writing kept the ideals of the loving-kindness meditation at the forefront of our mind. It was a regular reminder of who we wanted to be.

Keep in mind that the writing meditation is changing our views, and not eliminating them. Through our practice of mindfulness meditation, we're trying to see the true nature of reality, and not necessarily develop views about it. I think the greatest value in the exercise is that it can bring our views more in line with reality, and help us become the person we want to be. It will help us stay focused in our practice, so that we can continue to progress in our spiritual development.

When doing the writing meditation, there are two important things to remember. First, in order for the loving-kindness meditation to have a lasting effect, you need to practice it regularly for a period of time, for example, every day for a few months. I've made it part of my daily routine. Second, don't sacrifice the concentration/mindfulness meditation training for the writing meditation. If you neglect these, your progress will suffer and your insight will not deepen.

Track your progress with your meditation journal, and see how your demeanor is changing. That is, are you becoming less judgmental, and treating people with more loving-kindness? As you progress in your mindfulness meditation practice, the qualities described in the verses will come to you naturally. In Step 11, I'll show you how to use writing meditation for healing the wounds from your past.

See the appendix for a copy of the loving-kindness writing meditation. It includes detailed instructions for performing the exercise. For your convenience, I've made a printable version available on our website. In our upcoming *Mindfulness Meditation Workbook,* you'll find several writing meditations for overcoming a variety of issues, such as overeating, low self-esteem, substance abuse, and more.

## The Mindfulness Meditation Retreat: Your Most Powerful Tool

Many people just like you are committed to their meditation practice and want to advance it further. For this purpose, the mindfulness meditation retreat is the most powerful tool at your disposal. I am not exaggerating when I say that you can make years' worth of progress in just a matter of days. Of the people I know, the ones who are the most peaceful and emotionally secure are those who attend retreats regularly.

> Those who attend retreats regularly are generally more peaceful and emotionally secure.

Remember, the rate of your spiritual development is directly dependent upon your efforts—more specifically, right effort. The reason for this is that it's through our diligent effort that we connect with the vast ocean of mindfulness energy where our True Nature resides.

Throughout this book, I've stressed the importance of dwelling in the Three Jewels; the Buddha, the Dharma, and the Sangha. Until now, I've talked about how to incorporate them into your daily life as separate elements because they will enhance your practice. Now, imagine what it would be like to dwell deeply in all three at the same time, all day long, for several days straight. It would be one very powerful experience. Right?

When a group of people dwell in the Three Jewels at the same time, it produces a tremendous amount of mindfulness energy capable of healing and transforming everyone in ways you never imagined:

- I've seen people at a retreat who were painfully shy, be transformed into confident and outgoing people by the end of the retreat.

- I've seen other people who were haunted by painful traumas from their past, be freed from the pain and suffering, and forgive those who had harmed them.

- Some people have overcome tremendous guilt, shame, and remorse over their actions that harmed others.

- I've seen people attain a level of peace and serenity they had never experienced before.

All these changes took place in just a matter of five days. This is quite common to those who actively participate in the retreat program. That is, if you put in the effort, then you will achieve the results. Once you've been to a retreat, you'll see what you've been missing. That's what happened to me.

At a retreat, you will essentially be practicing like a monk, and therefore, achieve similar results:

- You will meditate with a large group three to four times a day, which amounts to about four to six hours of meditation daily.

- Without the usual demands of your life, it will be easier to practice mindfulness in all of your activities.

- You will also have direct access to a teacher to guide you through the practice, and answer any questions you may have.

The first retreat I attended was a 7-day retreat. We had two or three group meditation sessions a day, a dharma talk by Zen master Thich Nhat Hanh, and group discussion sessions where we talked about our experience, and asked questions of the monks and nuns. When I returned home, my friends and family members saw a noticeable difference in my demeanor. I was a lot more peaceful. In fact, I was so quiet that people kept asking me if something was wrong. In addition to my practice, the retreats have helped me in several other ways:

- I've developed greater self-confidence.
- I've improved my relationships. They're no longer filled with conflicts and power struggles.
- I am never lonely—even when I'm alone.
- I rarely get angry, and if I do, I know how to keep the anger from escalating and consuming me.
- I no longer have nightmares, because I've dealt with all the wounds from my past.
- I never get stressed out, or overwhelmed by life's challenges.
- Even my mental abilities have improved, such as memory and the ability to think clearly.

Now, not all retreats are the same. There are many retreats where you basically just listen to guest speakers talk about spirituality, and devote little time to meditation. These are OK, but they don't really give you the tools you need to keep making progress when you return home. The most effective retreats are the ones where you actually learn and practice the mindfulness meditation techniques.

If you truly want to get the most from your meditation practice, then you need to attend a retreat that teaches you the techniques that will give you a solid foundation of the mindfulness meditation practice. Otherwise, you'll miss out on the full benefits of the practice.

I recommend attending at least a 5-7 day retreat, because it takes a couple of days just to unwind. A weekend retreat is fine for getting a good introduction to the practice and getting you on the right track, but a weeklong retreat will give you the full power of the mindfulness meditation practice, and enable you to achieve dramatic results. It will save you years' worth of time and effort, especially if you attend a retreat regularly, such as once a year. Your friends and family will see a remarkable difference in you when you return home.

## Conclusion

In this step, you learned about the two most powerful tools of your practice: loving-kindness writing meditation, and the mindfulness meditation retreat. Both will enable you to make years' worth of progress in just a matter of days. The writing meditation will help you reprogram your subconscious, so that you begin practicing unconditional love without any conscious effort. It will come to you naturally.

The healing and transformational power of a mindfulness meditation retreat is much greater than what we're able to cultivate on our own, or at a weekly meditation meeting. Once you attend your first retreat, you'll see just how powerful it really is. The mindfulness meditation retreat will significantly shorten your path to enlightenment.

These tools are important because they will help you make the mindfulness meditation practice a way of life, and not just a part of your life. When this happens, your spiritual development will begin to accelerate, and you will gain an understanding of the human condition that few people achieve in their entire lives. And with this understanding will come great inner strength and serenity.

*"There is no happiness greater than the peace of nirvana."*

~ Buddha

The next step in our practice is the application of our developing wisdom. With wisdom, comes the responsibility to take mindful action to help ease the suffering in the world. We will begin with the practice of mindful consumption. In Step 10, we will examine how our consumption affects not only our own body and mind, but also the rest of the world.

As you progress in your spiritual development, you will see that true happiness and wisdom are indeed inseparable. You will develop unconditional love for all beings, as you realize that all are interconnected. With mindfulness, you will see that the happiness of one being contributes to the happiness of others, just as the suffering of one contributes to the suffering of others.

## Exercises

The following exercises will help you make years' worth of progress in a very short period of time—especially the writing meditation, and the mindfulness meditation retreat. You'll let go of unwholesome habits and become more outgoing and sociable, and they will happen naturally. I think you'll be amazed at how quickly you can transform your life and relationships.

**1. Practice concentration and mindfulness while performing routine activities.** These are great opportunities to practice our observation skills, instead of getting lost in unproductive thinking, such as worrying and fantasizing. Here are some ideas:

    a. **At home.** Making the bed, folding clothes, washing dishes, sweeping, vacuuming and any other cleaning activity, mowing the lawn, taking out the trash, and many others.

    b. **At work.** Filing, walking, straightening out the office or work area, and any other work-related task that doesn't require a great deal of thought.

As you gain some experience with the practice, you will begin using concentration and mindfulness in all your activities without any conscious effort.

**2. Practice living deeply in the present moment.** Begin questioning the true nature of time, and the present moment. You can do this in the following settings:

    a. While you are performing activities very mindfully

    b. When you have some downtime, and can sit for a few minutes contemplating

    c. Write down your observations in your meditation journal.

**3. Incorporate writing meditation into your daily routine.** Go to our website (http://www.MindfulnessMeditationInstitute.org) and download a printable copy of the loving-kindness writing meditation. Follow the instructions provided. If you don't have access to the Internet, you can find it in the appendix. I generally write two verses each day right before my sitting meditation session, but any time of the day will work.

**4.  If possible, attend a mindfulness meditation retreat.** Ideally, you'll want a retreat that has a good balance of instruction and time for meditation. Retreats like these are generally very limited and get booked up far in advance, so you may need to act quickly. I would recommend at least one retreat per year. If you would like more information about mindfulness meditation retreats, visit our website.

# STEP 10

## Mindful Consumption for Optimal Health and Performance

*Your body is precious. It is your vehicle for awakening. Treat it with care.*

~ BUDDHA

### Chapter Highlights

- Unmindful Consumption and the Illusion of Happiness
- Foods and Nutrients for Maximum Spiritual Growth
- Physical Activity for Optimal Performance of Body and Mind
- How to Lose Weight Mindfully
- Substance Use and the Perpetuation of Suffering
- Conclusion
- Exercises

**Step 10**  *"We became aware of how unmindful consumption perpet-uates our suffering, and prevents us from achieving true inner peace."*

E VER SINCE I WAS A YOUNG MAN, I've been interested in body-building. Though I never competed, I took my training seriously. I wanted to build the best physique possible. I quickly learned that in order to succeed, I needed to know a great deal about nutrition and physiology, and develop a deep awareness of what was happening in my body. I never realized the impact this would have on my spiritual development. It turned out to be a blessing.

We all want to live long and healthy lives, but few of us fully understand how our consumption affects our health. We usually make our consumption decisions based on our desires and emotions. We generally eat foods that taste good, or buy things that bring us pleasure, such as new clothes and jewelry. Few of us stop to think about whether the things we eat contain the nutrients our body and mind need for optimal health and performance. Oftentimes, it takes a serious illness to wake us up.

So why is our health important to our meditation practice? One reason is that our physical discomfort will make it difficult to concentrate and be mindful. When we're not

> *"Health is the greatest gift; contentment is the greatest wealth."*
>
> ~ BUDDHA

feeling well, we are distracted by our ailments, and this becomes an impediment to our spiritual development.

Another reason is that some of the nutrients and substances we put into our body can hinder our ability to develop mindfulness. For example, too much sugar can make us feel restless and anxious, and when it wears off, it can make us feel lethargic.

This is why it's so important to learn how our body functions—so we can provide it with the proper nutrients and physical activity necessary for optimal health and performance. If we are not able to keep our mind strong and clear, then we will lose our hard-earned spiritual growth.

Until now, we've only discussed issues related to the training of our mind. We've learned to become aware of the things that go into our mind in order to grow spiritually. In Step 10, we're going to look at how the things we put into our body affect our spiritual development.

In this step, you're going to learn about mindful consumption of nutrients and other substances, as well as the importance of physical activity. Then you'll be able to make healthier choices that will enhance your development. I am only going to discuss these topics in general because they can take several books to cover in-depth. However, I will provide you with the tools necessary for making mindful choices. I will also show you how to lose weight mindfully, and keep it off.

## Unmindful Consumption and the Illusion of Happiness

In Western society, we often avoid talking about issues related to our weight, or consumption of substances such as alcohol and tobacco. Whenever someone tells us that we're eating, drinking, or smoking too much, we usually become defensive. We sometimes avoid dealing with these issues until they become life-threatening, but by then, most of the damage is already done. Sadly, many people never address these problems, and eventually die from the harmful consequences to their health.

Overcoming unmindful consumption can be challenging. It's not simply a matter of knowing how some substances adversely affect us, but also having the inner strength to make healthier choices. In one of the twelve-step fellowships, they have a saying that describes the problem well. It says, "Lack of power is our dilemma." In other words, lack of mindfulness is our dilemma. This means that in order to overcome unmindful consumption, we need to raise our level of mindfulness energy. That is, we need to build our inner strength, which is exactly what we're doing through our practice.

We also need something else: healthy coping skills. When we're unhappy, we often try covering up our pain with some form of sensual pleasure. We usually get pleasure from things such as eating, smoking, drinking alcohol, and sometimes using illicit drugs. However, indulging in these forms of pleasure-seeking not only perpetuate our suffering, but they also create more problems. Though most of us learn coping skills as we're growing up, some of us do not.

Regardless of how much we engage in pleasure-seeking, there is always a spiritual consequence, because this behavior is simply a manifestation of the hindrances of sensual desire and aversion. Certainly, none of us want to feel pain, but remember that happiness through sensual pleasure is short-lived.

Through our mindfulness meditation practice, we're trying to achieve long-lasting peace and serenity by eliminating the root causes of our suffering. We do this by confronting and then transforming them so that they don't trigger painful emotions—not by avoiding them with a dull or distracted mind. So if we want to be free of our pain and suffering, we must become willing to stop consuming substances that bring us only temporary relief, and deal with our problems in a healthy manner.

## Foods and Nutrients for Maximum Spiritual Growth

There is a big misconception about the Buddha, which sometimes leads to confusion about mindful consumption. Contrary to popular belief, the Buddha was not obese. Many people associate the Buddha with images of a fat bald man often seen wearing a robe and carrying a cloth sack. This is not the historical Buddha of whom we've been referring to in our discussions. The fat bald man is actually called Budai. He was a Chinese Zen monk who lived around 900 CE. He is mainly a folklore figure that has become part of a number of Buddhist and Taoist traditions.

The historical Buddha was Siddhartha Gautama, the young prince who achieved enlightenment through meditation. Buddha was the title given to him after he achieved enlightenment. It means "The Awakened One." The historical accounts depict him as a tall slender man who advocated mindful consumption, which is an integral part of his teachings, and plays a vital role in our development of mindfulness.

Our body and mind need certain nutrients to function properly. However, few of us have a good understanding of what we need for optimal performance. A recent study found that many of us approach our consumption of nutrients by eating things that appeal to us, rather than how they affect us. So what happens is that our body is constantly trying to compensate for the resulting malnutrition. Furthermore, if we're overweight, we sometimes try cutting our calories, which leads to further malnutrition because in the process, we end up cutting back on essential nutrients.

Mindful consumption is an understanding of how nutrients affect our body, and making informed choices about which ones to consume, how much to consume, and when to consume them. Many of us rely on other people to provide us with a diet plan that we can follow blindly, without understanding the reasoning behind it. And when we get tired of it, we either look for another one, or go back to eating the way we did before our diet.

If we want to be mindful of our health, we should at least have a basic understanding of nutrition. Then we can make informed decisions about what our body needs for optimal health and performance. This way, healthy consumption of nutrients becomes a way of life, and not a diet.

## Basic Nutrition

I'm sure many of you already have some understanding of basic nutrition. But for the benefit of those who don't, I will give you an overview of some of the fundamental principles. An understanding of basic nutrition is important if you want to make better choices in your diet, because these choices will affect not only your health, but also your spiritual development.

There are four basic types of nutrients that our body needs to function properly: protein, carbohydrates, fat, vitamins and minerals, and water. These are nutrients that we depend on not only for survival, but also for optimal health and performance.

## Protein

Protein is the building block of body tissue. Our body needs protein to build and repair tissue. Everyday, cells in our body die and are replaced by new ones. Each time this happens, our body requires protein to create the new cells. Children require large amounts of protein to foster their rapid physical development. We may also need large amounts of protein after an injury, or surgery. If we do not consume enough protein, then our recuperation will take much longer. It is like building a house without sufficient materials.

Though most foods contain protein, meats are the primary source. You can find high quantities of protein in beef, poultry, fish, and dairy products. Fruits and vegetables also contain protein, but in much smaller quantities.

Protein is made of complex molecules called amino acids. Each source of protein has a slightly different amino acid profile. The body needs certain amino acids in order to carry out its functions. There is a group of them called the essential amino acids. They are considered essential to our diet because our body cannot manufacture them.

If the body does not receive the essential amino acids through diet, then it will have to do without, therefore, compromising the body's performance. This is a common problem among vegetarians because vegetables and legumes do not contain all of them. If they want to get all the essential amino acids through their diet, then they need to eat certain combinations of foods to ensure adequate supply. Another option is to add an amino acid supplement to their diet.

## Carbohydrates

Carbohydrates provide our body with energy. Every activity that our body performs requires energy. We need energy for muscle movement, and for our organs to function properly. There are two basic types of carbohydrates: complex and simple. Complex carbohydrates provide us with a steady stream of energy, and simple carbohydrates will give us a quick burst.

Our primary sources of complex carbohydrates are starches, such as potatoes, bread, and whole grains. Simple carbohydrates are essentially sugars, which can be found naturally in most fruits. Pure sugar is extracted from the sugar cane, and used in sweet drinks and desserts.

## Fat

Fats are another source of energy. They are slightly different than carbohydrates in the sense that they can be stored for much longer periods. Stored fat is broken down by the body when there aren't enough carbohydrates available. Fat also helps insulate the body organs against shock, and regulate body temperature. The main sources of fat are red meat, poultry, and dairy products.

Our body needs protein, carbohydrates, and fat in certain proportions in order for it to function properly. The Institute of Medicine recommends the following distribution of calories for adults:

- Protein: 10-35% of total calories
- Carbohydrates: 45-65%
- Fat: 20-35%

As you can see, most of our calories should come from carbohydrates, mainly complex carbohydrates. We should limit our intake of fat because too much can lead to obesity, clogged arteries, and heart disease. The foods with the highest content of fat are fried foods, which we should try to avoid as much as possible.

You generally want to spread out your calories into 5-6 meals each day. For example, have your three main meals (breakfast, lunch, and dinner) and a couple of snacks in between. This will ensure that your body has a steady stream of nutrients. If you go long periods without eating, then you force your body to break down healthy tissue in order to find the protein and energy necessary for your body's primary functions.

## Vitamins and Minerals

Vitamins and minerals are a set of diverse chemical compounds that help facilitate various bodily functions. Some vitamins, such as D, help regulate tissue growth and differentiation. Other vitamins, such as E, act as antioxidants. That is, they remove from the body certain chemical compounds that cause cell damage. The B vitamins are instrumental in cell metabolism (the transportation of energy molecules).

Vitamins and minerals are found in a variety of sources. They're not restricted to certain classes of foods. It may be a challenge to get the necessary amounts, even in a well-balanced diet, so it would be a good idea to supplement your diet with a good multivitamin. Some are specifically formulated for different age groups and levels of physical activity, so choose one that is most suitable for your needs.

## Water

Water is another vital nutrient. It is essential for just about every metabolic process. It is also involved in transporting chemical byproducts out of the body. Since it cannot be stored, we must replenish it frequently.

Dehydration is a common problem among older adults. Insufficient water intake can lead to a variety of health problems. Fatigue is usually the first sign of dehydration. Other symptoms include headaches, rapid heartbeat, moodiness, feeling lightheaded or dizzy, digestive problems, constipation, allergies, wrinkles, and sagging skin.

Some researchers argue that good hydration can aid in the cure of arthritis, back pain, angina, migraines, colitis, asthma, high blood pressure, adult-onset diabetes, high cholesterol, heartburn, depression, and much more. I have seen people overcome many heath problems just from drinking more water. In one case, a friend's arthritis disappeared completely. The stiffness in her knees apparently was caused by lack of lubrication.

So, how much water do you need? The Institute of Medicine recommends that men drink roughly 3 liters (about 13 cups) of total beverages a day. Women should get about 2.2 liters (about 9 cups) of total beverages a day. I know this sounds like a lot, but it's necessary for your body to function at an optimal level. What I do is keep several glasses of water throughout the house, and I take a couple of sips each time I pass by one of them.

Nutrition is a bit more complex than I've just described, but I think this overview gives you a broad understanding of the nutritional requirements for a healthy body and mind. If you would like to learn more, I recommend *Nutrition For Dummies* by Carol Ann Rinzler. She explains the basics in layman terms. Nutrition and fitness magazines are also good sources of information, and they will help you stay motivated to eating healthy.

## Sugar: Friend or Foe?

Sugar is part of a normal diet. We need it for our energy requirements. However, excessive sugar intake can have adverse side effects. Sugar gets into our bloodstream in the form of glucose. Too much of it can make us feel restless and anxious, like we're having an anxiety attack. If we consume it right before bed, we'll have difficulty sleeping and have strange dreams, or even nightmares.

To give you an example, a friend of mine called me one day and asked me to help her figure out the reason for her anxiety that day. She was expecting some kind of spiritual insight into the cause. As she told me about her day, she mentioned that she had been eating cake all afternoon. Somebody at work had a birthday, and her coworkers got her a cake.

Later in the conversation, she told me about the meditation meeting she attended that evening, and how she had trouble relaxing and felt a terrible anxiety throughout the whole session. I asked her, "Didn't you say you ate cake all afternoon?" She slowly replied, "Yes." So I said to her, "That's why you're feeling so anxious. Your body is struggling to burn off all the excess sugar in your bloodstream."

We all experience spikes in our sugar level occasionally. It usually happens right after we eat, and how much depends on the glycemic index of the foods we consume. The glycemic index is essentially a measure of how fast and how high a particular food can raise our blood sugar. Foods that have a high glycemic index are desserts, candy, and many soft drinks.

We generally want our foods to provide us with a steady stream of energy, in addition to other nutrients. We don't want quick bursts because they will have an equal and opposite reaction. That is, our blood sugar will go too low and make us feel lethargic and sleepy, and this is not conducive to mindfulness either.

So then, what can you do if you get a spike in your blood sugar? A little physical activity will remedy the situation: a short walk, push-ups, sit-ups, or any other exercise you like. About two or three minutes of exercise is sufficient to draw the sugar from your bloodstream. So if you're having trouble sleeping because your blood sugar is high, then walk for a couple of minutes inside your house. You'll sleep much better the rest of the night.

## Food Allergies

Other nutrients can also have a dramatic impact on our ability to function properly. Some of us are allergic to certain food additives, such as monosodium glutamate (MSG). It gives me a headache and makes me very lethargic. The way to find out if you're allergic to certain foods is to pay close attention to how you feel after you eat. If you have some kind of reaction, you'll have to do some investigating and/or see a doctor.

It takes a great deal of mindfulness to determine the cause of a food allergy, because there are so many possibilities. It's difficult for a physician to make a diagnosis because he would need to be aware of just about every aspect of your life.

Sometimes people are never able to find the root cause of an allergy. To give you an example, my father suffered from migraines much of his life. He went to all kinds of doctors to try to have the condition diagnosed. He even went to the Mayo Clinic, but nobody ever found the cause of his migraines. When I realized that MSG was causing my headaches, I thought about my deceased father: maybe he had been getting migraines for the same reason I was.

## Physical Activity for Optimal Performance of Body and Mind

Over the last few decades, we've seen a growing weight problem throughout the world. In the United States, obesity has reached critical levels. In our personal lives, a weight problem isn't something we can simply ignore and not expect to suffer the consequences, to our health and our spiritual development.

The underlying causes of obesity are the recent advancements in technology. These advances have led to more sedentary lifestyles. They have changed the way we work and play. Work-related tasks that used to require physical activities are now being handled more efficiently by computers and other electronic devices.

Our forms of entertainment activities have also changed. The growth of cable television and video games has translated into people spending more time in front of the TV, and less time engaged in physical activities.

The other area where technological advancements have contributed to the obesity problem is food production. Suppliers are finding ways to produce more food at lower costs. Many of the foods that are being produced today are higher in calories, but lower in nutritional value.

Physical activity is essential for optimal health and performance of our body and mind. One way it improves the performance of our mind is by increasing the flow of blood to the brain, because it is through the blood that our brain receives the nutrients it needs to function properly. Physical activity also prevents us from gaining too much weight, which can lead to health problems, such as diabetes, heart disease, and stroke. It will even help you live longer.

## A Little Exercise Can Go a Long Way

Many people think they have to spend hours in the gym in order to be healthy. That isn't necessarily so. According to a recent study, you can achieve significant health benefits from just a few minutes of exercise. Here are some ways you can improve your health significantly without spending a lot of time in the gym:

**Time:** 12 minutes
**Frequency:** Five days a week
**Exercise:** Moderate-intensity cardio, such as walking or climbing stairs
**Result:** Lower your risk of heart attack and stroke by 27 percent.
**How:** Aerobic activity reduces bad cholesterol, raises good cholesterol, and improves blood pressure and circulation.

**Time:** 2 minutes
**Frequency:** Five days a week
**Exercise:** Resistance-band exercise
**Result:** Reduces muscle pain by 37 percent, and headaches by 43 percent.
**How:** The exercise increases blood flow and oxygen to the muscles.

**Time:** 10 minutes
**Frequency:** Once a day
**Exercise:** Vigorous biking or running.
**Result:** Helps ward off stress and obesity.

| | |
|---|---|
| **How:** | The exercise burns fat, preserves muscle, and increases insulin sensitivity. |

| | |
|---|---|
| **Time:** | 25 minutes |
| **Frequency:** | As needed |
| **Exercise:** | Non-weight bearing exercise, such as stationary bicycle. |
| **Result:** | Reduces physical pain by 28 percent. |
| **How:** | Disrupts the neurotransmitters that communicate pain. |

| | |
|---|---|
| **Time:** | 15 minutes |
| **Frequency:** | Three times a week |
| **Exercise:** | Any moderate-intensity exercise, such as walking. |
| **Result:** | Helps reduce the risk of dementia by 38 percent. |
| **How:** | Improves circulation and health of the blood vessels in the brain. |

Source: Melinda Dodd, *Too Busy to Exercise? Try These 6 Quick-Fix Workouts,* More Magazine, December 2011/January 2012, http://www.more.com/quick-workouts-for-busy-women

As you can see, you have a variety of choices for incorporating a little exercise into your life. Just a few minutes of exercise several times a week can have tremendous health benefits. All the exercises described above increase blood circulation in the brain, and improve mental capacity. This is good news for spiritual seekers wanting to improve their concentration and mindfulness.

## How to Lose Weight Mindfully

Do you struggle to keep your weight under control? If so, you're not alone. We hear every day on the news about how a growing number of Americans are overweight. At the personal level, the main culprit is unmindful eating. According to Brian Wansink, director of the Cornell University Food and Brand Laboratory, much of our eating is influenced by unconscious triggers, such as:

- Room temperature and lighting
- How much the people we are with consume
- Whether or not we're watching television
- How visible foods are
- The shapes and sizes of plates and cups, and more

In one study conducted by Wansink, participants were asked to serve themselves ice cream as they wished. The study found that those who used a bigger bowl served themselves and ate 31 percent more. And those that used a larger serving utensil ate 57 percent more. According to Wansink, the majority of our eating decisions are automatic. And to further compound the problem, we are more suscep-tible to unconscious triggers when we're under stress.

> Losing weight is not complicated. You simply need to burn more calories than you consume.

The reason we're not fully aware of our eating is because we lack the skills to eat mindfully. When we're eating, our mind is often on something else, and we're not paying attention to what we're eating, or how much. Our stress and anxiety prevent us from being in the present moment, which is where eating is always taking place. And if we have a weight problem, we usually try not to think about how much we're eating.

Losing weight is not complicated. You simply need to burn more calories than you consume. It really is that simple. This means that you must decrease your calories and increase your physical activity. However, it takes mindfulness to put this basic principle into practice.

The reason many people have trouble losing weight is because they only address one part of an exercise and nutrition regimen. They either cut their calories without increasing their exercise, or they increase their exercise without cutting their calories. Both scenarios will backfire on you because of the way the body adapts to changes in caloric intake and physical activity.

When you cut your calories drastically, your body goes into survival mode and tries to conserve energy by operating at a lower energy level. In other words, your metabolism slows down. Then, if you temporarily increase your calories, such as when you go out to dinner or attend a function, your body will store the majority of the calories you consume.

If you lose weight by cutting your calories drastically, much of the weight loss will be valuable muscle mass, which further slows your metabolism because now you've lost your energy burning capability. When you eventually gain the weight back, it will most likely be fat, and you'll end up more out of shape than before. This is why many people gain weight when they cut their calories.

If you exercise while cutting your calories, then you'll speed up your metabolism, and you'll preserve your muscle mass and burn fat more quickly. You will also need to increase your protein intake. There are two reasons for this: (1) your body will need more protein to build muscle, and (2) the protein itself will help speed up your metabolism slightly.

Now, if you increase your exercise without either reducing or maintaining the same calories, you'll also gain weight. The reason is that when you exercise, your body requires more energy to repair itself, and therefore, you become hungrier. Then, if you eat according to your hunger, you will increase your calories, and you'll gain weight because you will still be consuming more calories than you're burning. This is why people are often baffled when they're working out like crazy, and never able to lose weight.

Both of these reactions are survival mechanisms that we've developed through the evolution of our species. They are designed to help us survive adverse conditions regarding our safety and food supply. So, if you want to lose weight in a healthy manner, you need to consistently burn more calories than you consume. It's much better to do it steadily, instead of taking drastic measures. Losing one or two pounds a week is easily achievable for most people.

Keep in mind that you will have to allow yourself to be hungry for a little while before you eat. Most people are accustomed to eating as soon as they get hungry. If you do this, then you never give your body a chance to burn the stored calories. On the other hand, if you go too long without eating, then your body starts burning lean body mass. It's a delicate balance.

> A recent study published in the Journal of American Dietetic Association found a direct link between mindfulness and weight loss.

One formula that works well for me when trying to lose weight is to consume enough calories at each meal so that I am hungry for about an hour before my next meal. For example, if you eat every four hours, then consume enough calories to last you three hours. This will force your body to use stored energy for that last hour. If you are doing cardiovascular exercise as part of your regimen, then that stored energy burned will most likely be fat.

There is some good news for those of you who are diligent with your mindfulness meditation practice. A recent study published in the Journal of American Dietetic Association found a direct link between mindfulness and weight loss. The participants who were trained to be more mindful of their eating habits and to examine their views about eating, were more likely to lose weight.

Now that you're developing mindfulness through your meditation practice, you'll begin eating more mindfully. However, you can take this to a much higher level with writing meditation. Remember how effective loving-kindness writing meditation was in dramatically changing your attitudes about other people? Well, now we're going to use the same approach to help you change your attitude about nutrition, and to help keep your weight under control. We've developed a writing meditation specifically for mindful consumption. This writing meditation will allow mindful eating to come to you naturally:

- **You will lose weight effortlessly.** Mindful eating and physical activity will come to you naturally.

- **You will feel better physically.** You will have more energy and fewer health problems. Eating healthy will result in better overall physical well-being.

- **You will feel better mentally.** When you provide your brain with the nutrients it needs for optimal performance, your memory and cognitive abilities will improve.

- **You will feel better emotionally.** Your confidence and self-esteem will increase because you will know that you're taking good care of yourself.

- **You will finally be in control.** With mindfulness, you'll be in control of your eating decisions, and much less susceptible to unconscious triggers.

But in order to achieve control, it is vital to remain diligent and committed to your mindfulness meditation practice. Mindful consumption writing meditation will be most effective in helping you develop mindful eating habits in the short-run, and sitting meditation will give you the inner strength necessary for making better choices for long-term health.

Remember how easy writing meditation is? You simply copy the meditation by hand in a notebook for about 10-15 minutes a day. In just a few days, you'll find yourself naturally becoming aware of your eating behavior. You'll start letting go of behaviors that aren't serving you well, and replace them with ones that will help you achieve your goals of optimal health and performance. You can find a copy of the mindful consumption writing meditation in the appendix. You can also download a printable copy from the Resources section of our website.

## Substance Use and the Perpetuation of Suffering

Now we're going to talk about our consumption of other substances such as alcohol, tobacco, and illicit drugs. I realize this can be a sensitive issue because some of us depend on these substances to help us relax and deal with stress. While they can help us relax some, the way they do it presents a major obstacle to our spiritual development. If we want to continue growing, we must have the courage to give them up. Otherwise, we'll miss out on a whole new level of peace and serenity.

Each substance works a bit differently to help us relax. But, in general, they either cause our body to release endorphins to make us feel good, or they prevent the proper functioning of our brain, so that we can't recall unpleasant memories. They essentially dull our mind, and this is certainly not conducive to mindfulness. Over time, the use of these substances will have a cumulative effect, and will greatly diminish our ability to concentrate and our memory, especially short-term memory.

With some substances, such as tobacco products, the physical dependence becomes the cause of much of our anxiety, and only by ingesting more of the substance do we gain relief. They can be more of a challenge to overcome because the withdrawal symptoms can be quite uncomfortable. In such cases, you will most likely need help.

These substances not only perpetuate our suffering, but they also make it worse. By continuing to consume them, we never allow ourselves to heal because we continually avoid dealing with the root causes of our suffering. Many people do overcome their painful memories, and they do it without the use of substances. Though some memories may be difficult to confront, we must confront them without numbing our emotions, if we're going to overcome them.

If you're having difficulty giving up a substance on your own, I would encourage you to seek help. There is nothing to be ashamed of by admitting that you need help. There are various twelve-step programs with people who have experienced the same challenges, and they've overcome their substance use by helping each other. There are many wonderful people there who are more than happy to help you. They can guide you through the process, but it requires a desire and willingness on your part. I've seen many people overcome their dependence on drugs and alcohol, and go on to live happy and fulfilling lives. There is no reason to go it alone.

> Once we stop using substances to help us relax, our spiritual development will progress much faster.

Some people use these substances in moderation. While they may not create problems in their lives, they will prevent them from growing spiritually and emotionally. They will soon reach a plateau, and be unable to reach a higher level until they give them up, whether their use is occasional or daily.

Some prescription medications, such as anti-depressants, tranquilizers, sleep aids, and pain medications, can also present obstacles to our spiritual and emotional development. In such cases, you would need to consult with your doctor to determine if the medications are necessary. Sometimes we're prescribed these medications for a temporary condition, but our body becomes physically dependent on them, making it difficult to stop.

This is a delicate situation, and you should always follow the advice of your doctor. Also, use your mindfulness to help you see whether you truly need these medications. If you and your doctor determine that the medications are not essential, then ask him how to quit.

Keep in mind that the incentives in the health care system are not geared toward providing treatments for optimal health. Practitioners are in business, or employed by organizations, to make a profit just like any other business. Ultimately, it is our responsibility to make good decisions regarding our health, which is another way of putting our mindfulness into action. Once we stop using substances to help us relax, our spiritual development will progress much faster.

## Conclusion

In Step 10, we discussed some of the behaviors that will slow your progress, and what you can do to overcome them. You learned the basics of good nutrition for optimal health and performance of body and mind. You also learned how physical activity plays an important role in your spiritual development.

*"To keep the body in good health is a duty... otherwise we shall not be able to keep our mind strong and clear."*

~ Unknown

You are investing a great deal of effort in your meditation practice, and you certainly don't want to compromise your hard-earned spiritual growth. Unfortunately, many of our behaviors do just that. It's like trying to fill a leaky bucket. We're losing much of what we've worked so hard for.

We often hear spiritual seekers talk about the interdependence of mind, body, and spirit. However, few of them emphasize the importance of mindful consumption, and how it affects their body and spiritual growth. If you truly want to reach a higher level of spirituality, then you must leave no stone unturned. This includes your health. Otherwise, your growth will always be limited.

In Step 11, you'll learn how to eliminate even more obstacles, and in Step 12, I'll show you how carrying the message to other people will further enhance your development. The objective is to put your practice on the fast track toward your goal of long-lasting inner peace.

## Exercises

The exercises below will help you learn how to make better choices regarding your health and nutrition. Not only will they improve your physical, mental, and emotional health, but they will also enhance your spiritual development.

**1. Writing meditation.** Whether or not you have a weight problem, this exercise will help you practice mindful consumption. Go to the Resource section of our website and download a printable copy of the mindful consumption writing meditation. Copy the meditation by hand in a notebook every day for about 10-15 minutes. After a few days, begin writing a few notes in your meditation journal regarding your changing attitudes about health and nutrition, as well as any changes in your behavior.

2.  **Practicing mindful consumption.** For the next week, each time you ingest a nutrient or substance, pay close attention to how you feel afterward. Ask yourself what effect it's having on you physically, mentally, emotionally, and spiritually. Write down some of your observations in your meditation journal. I would suggest doing some research on their effects. This can give you some idea of what to look for. There is a wealth of information on the Internet that will help you. Just remember to use reliable sources in your research.

3.  **Learn the basics of health and nutrition** to develop an understanding of how your mind and body work, so you can make more mindful choices on the nutrients to consume for optimal health. I recommend *Nutrition For Dummies* by Carol Ann Rinzler. It explains the basics in layman terms. Health magazines also contain valuable information on relevant topics, and the latest research findings.

4.  **Prepare your own diet plan.** Once you have a basic understanding of health and nutrition, create your own diet plan based on your particular needs. I would suggest that you consult your doctor or dietitian, so he can give you some guidance. It would also be a good idea to have him give you feedback on your plan when it's finished.

5.  **Physical activity.** If you aren't already active, incorporate moderate physical activity into your daily routine. While a regular exercise program at a gym is great, it's not a requirement for optimal health. Develop a plan for exercise and put it in writing:

- Incorporate walking into your daily activities.
- Use the stairs whenever possible.
- Perform light lifting through activities at home and at work.

If you have physical limitations, then you will need to find alternate ways of getting some exercise. You will just need to be a little creative, and mindful.

**6. Strive to become free of alcohol, tobacco, and unnecessary medications.** These substances will prevent you from attaining true inner peace. If necessary, seek help from others who have given them up. Twelve-step programs are very effective at helping people quit the use of such substances. With regard to prescription medications, seek the advice of your doctor before making any adjustments. At the same time, make sure he helps you determine if the medications are necessary, and how you can give them up if they're not.

# STEP 11

## How to Find Freedom from Your Past with Mindfulness Meditation

*Loving oneself is the foundation for loving another person.*

            ~ THICH NHAT HANH

### Chapter Highlights

- The Causes of Our Painful Memories
- The Healing Power of Mindfulness Energy
- When Painful Memories Arise...
- The Sangha: An Indispensable Tool for Healing and Transformation
- Overcoming the Pain with Writing Meditation
- The Healing Power of a Retreat
- Conclusion
- Exercises

**Step 11**   *"With the strength, courage, and mindfulness we attained through our meditation practice, we confronted and overcame the wounds from our past."*

EARLY IN MY SPIRITUAL JOURNEY, my mentor had me confront the wounds from my past. He knew that they were major sources of my pain and suffering, and that I could not be truly free until they healed. He also taught me that even though I may have had good reasons to blame others for my suffering, it was unrealistic for me to expect anyone else to repair the damage. Therefore, it became my responsibility.

Some of us carry deep wounds in our heart, many of them from our childhood. We often try avoiding them, so that we don't re-live the pain and suffering. If we haven't learned constructive ways of dealing with them, then we've learned destructive ways.

Many of the behaviors we engage in to help us relax are merely ways to avoid thinking about the things that bother us. Or, they disrupt the normal functioning of our brain so that the painful memories are not accessed. This is especially true of drugs and alcohol. They give us a false sense of well-being.

The wounds from our past are significant obstacles to our spiritual and emotional development. If we keep avoiding them, we'll continue experiencing the pain and suffering, and never achieve the inner peace we're searching for.

> *"Everything is either an opportunity to grow, or an obstacle to keep you from growing. You get to choose."*
>
> ~ WAYNE W. DYER

In Step 11, you'll find out how to heal the wounds from your past using some of the practices you've already learned. I'll show you how to make the healing process as easy and painless as possible. You'll see how liberating it is to finally be free of your painful memories.

It takes a great deal of mindfulness energy to heal the wounds from our past. When you begin to confront them, you'll need to be strong enough so that you're not consumed by your emotions. Therefore, you'll need to rely heavily on your sources of mindfulness energy—the Three Jewels.

As you gain experience with your meditation practice, some old memories will rise to your conscious mind. But don't worry, because by then you should be strong enough to confront them. As your mindfulness develops, you'll be able to see your painful memories with much greater clarity, so you can transform them, and diminish their effect on you.

## The Causes of Our Painful Memories

Most of the wounds from our childhood revolve around our relationships (or lack of relationships) with our parents. For some of us, our spiritual connections with them were either very weak, were completely severed at some point, or maybe never existed. This can have significant implications for our ability to cope with conflicts when we're adults.

In a normal upbringing, both our parents are nurturing and emotionally available. With their guidance, we learn to deal with conflict (both internal and external) and to develop healthy relationships with a network of friends. But for many of us, this is not the case. Some of us grew up with parents who were emotionally and spiritually unavailable for various reasons: they were separated, deceased, or simply not the nurturing type. In some cases, our parents were unavailable because they were emotionally dysfunctional. For example, they were addicts or alcoholics, or may have been mentally ill.

Sometimes, separation from our parents is due to unusual circumstances. In my case, I was sent to live with my grandparents in Chile when I was 8 years old. During the 3 years I was there, my parents were separated.

If we don't receive the necessary nurturing and guidance from our parents, then we never develop the social skills needed to form healthy relationships with other people. Instead, we grow up feeling lost and disconnected from the rest of humanity. We begin to see life as a struggle between us and them. We also don't learn healthy coping skills, so we develop unwholesome behaviors to cope with our painful emotions.

These behaviors usually come in the form of power struggles to get the upper hand in our interactions or relationships with other people. We do this by getting them to accept our point of view, so we feel more in control and gain more leverage in getting what we want.

The problem with these types of interactions is that we gain an uplift at the expense of others—that is, we weaken them spiritually. Since this uplift is weak and short-lived, we need to keep engaging in power struggles in order to feel normal. These behaviors simply perpetuate the pain and suffering, not just in ourselves, but in those around us. This is a painful and lonely existence.

## The Healing Power of Mindfulness Energy

So how do you heal the wounds from your past? By raising your mindfulness energy through your meditation practice, you'll become strong enough to transform the memories so that they don't trigger the painful emotions. You will also gain much greater clarity, which will enable you to see the true nature of the circumstances that created the wounds in your heart. Soon, the pain and suffering will simply disappear.

> *"If you have no compassion for yourself, then you are not capable of developing compassion for others."*
>
> ~ Dalai Lama

With greater understanding, we can begin to see those who victimized us through the eyes of compassion. We will see that they were also victims of traumatic events, and learned to cope with their feelings by inflicting pain and suffering on others. This will help us forgive them, which will further diminish the power of our painful memories.

In cases where there is no specific person to blame, we often blame everyone, including God and ourselves. As you develop mindfulness, you'll be able to look at past events more objectively, and see how blaming serves no useful purpose.

Overcoming our painful memories is pretty straightforward. In fact, it's not too difficult to overcome most of them through our meditation practice. I can illustrate how this works with a personal experience, about my relationship with my father.

My father essentially abandoned my family when my three sisters and I were children. For some reason, he didn't feel responsible for our upbringing. My parents divorced when I was around 11 years old, and I lost contact with my father for several years.

During that time, I became friends with one of our neighbors, who was about the same age as me. He and his father always did things together, such as play ball or go on vacation. For me, it was a constant reminder of my father's absence.

When my father finally did contact us, he acted as if we were the ones who had abandoned him. I thought he was completely out of touch with reality. I resented him for many years, but the resentment dissipated as I grew older. Still, I didn't have much interest in establishing a relationship with him, and he wondered why.

One day, while I was meditating, I had a profound spiritual awakening. I was 34 years old at the time. As a result of the experience, I became highly energized spiritually, which enabled me to go through a dramatic transformation. I became much more peaceful and compassionate. I felt like all my anger was gone.

This experience prompted me to take another look at my relationship with my father, and I saw that I still carried a resentment toward him. Then the most amazing thing happened. Within just a matter of seconds, the resentment completely evaporated, and was replaced with love and compassion for him. I began to see that he carried his own wounds from his childhood. I remembered that his father was very abusive with him, and therefore, he was simply a victim of his upbringing. Sadly, he never learned how to deal with the wounds from his past.

These insights enabled me to forgive my father and be at peace, and to be by his side in his remaining years. It no longer mattered what he had done to me. What mattered was that he was a person who suffered, and was just as deserving of loving-kindness as anyone else.

I realize that not everyone will have a profound spiritual awakening, but that's OK. Making steady progress is just as good. If you remain diligent and committed to your mindfulness meditation practice and implement the tools you've learned in this book, you'll become strong enough to overcome the wounds from your past.

## When Painful Memories Arise...

As you progress in your practice, your mind will become clearer and calmer. When this happens, memories of the past will arise during your meditation sessions, and some of them may be painful. This is a normal part of the healing process, so simply allow them to rise to the surface. By this time, you'll have the strength and the courage to confront them.

> Our painful emotions are rooted in our ego.

Remember that our painful emotions are rooted in our ego. As we become more connected with the rest of humanity, our True Nature will emerge and our ego will begin to diminish, as will our painful emotions.

When you reach this point, you will have developed the wisdom to see things more realistically. Old memories will look different because you'll be looking at them from a more mature perspective. Now that your observation skills are developing, you'll be able to look deeper into the circumstances that brought about those painful memories. You'll see that those who had harmed you were themselves suffering, and their actions were the result of their unmindfulness. So let the memories come up, and begin looking at them more objectively, like an outside observer.

This is a good time to make use of your meditation journal. Writing about painful situations will help you organize your thoughts. If you leave them floating around in your mind, they'll remain scrambled and unresolved. By writing down your thoughts, you'll see them more objectively, and finally be able to accept them and gain closure. This will also help you later when you review those entries. You'll see just how much you've grown.

## The Sangha: An Indispensable Tool for Healing and Transformation

Remember that our spiritual development greatly depends on how deeply we dwell in the Three Jewels. In this section, you'll discover how the sangha can be instrumental in helping you overcome your painful memories. I realize some people would prefer to meditate alone. While meditating alone is an important element of our practice, if you don't practice with others, you'll be depriving yourself of the healing power of the sangha.

Many of us are raised to solve our problems without anyone's help. This attitude stems from pride and/or fear. There is no reason to continue suffering when there are many caring people willing and able to help us work through our problems. Many friends and strangers helped me when I was struggling. Now I help others who are walking the same path.

The sangha is absolutely vital when dealing with your past. Without it, your progress in this area will be very slow and limited. I can always tell when people have attempted this on their own. When I talk to them, they usually talk about how they're struggling with issues that they should have overcome years ago.

People who are involved in a sangha and are diligent with their meditation practice, overcome their painful issues very quickly. There are several ways that a sangha will make it much easier:

- **It is a resource of mindfulness energy.** By practicing with others, we generate more energy than we would by practicing alone. I notice a significant difference in my ability to be mindful when I attend my sangha regularly.

- **It is a resource of valuable experience and wisdom.** More experienced members can share with us how they've overcome similar problems.

- **We can share our struggles with others.** When we share our concerns with the sangha, it diminishes their power over us. At my sangha, we dedicate a few minutes during each session for members to share their joys and concerns.

- **It keeps our mind occupied.** When we're dealing with a problem, we often make it worse by dwelling on it. We can prevent this by getting involved in helping other members.

- **Camaraderie.** It is comforting to know that we're not alone in our struggles. Everyone at the sangha has his own problems, and we help each other overcome them.

Another way a sangha can be instrumental in our spiritual development is through the use of a teacher, or mentor. A mentor is someone who has more experience than you, and can guide you in your meditation practice and through the healing process. He is someone you can confide in, and can give you advice on how to apply the practice to your everyday life.

Your mentor will help you make sense of the situations that created your painful memories. It's likely that he has overcome similar challenges, and this can be very comforting. With a mentor, you'll also learn to connect with another person on a much deeper level, and this will be instrumental in learning to have more intimate relationships with others, including family members. Over time, your relationship with your mentor will grow, and you'll develop a deep level of trust in him.

Some sanghas don't have mentors you can use in this manner. If you're already a member of a sangha, you may want to suggest at one of your business meetings that they incorporate the practice. It doesn't have to be anything formal. All it takes is for experienced members to let newer members know that they're available for guidance in the mindfulness meditation practice. It would also be a good idea to recommend to newcomers that they find a mentor to guide them through the practice.

At the very least, you can take it upon yourself to be available to members with less experience than yourself. You already have valuable experience to share with others. Even if you've been practicing for only a week, you can help someone who's been practicing for one day. That person will be grateful for your help.

In Step 12, we'll talk more about mentoring, but for now start thinking about how you can incorporate mentorship into your practice. It's essential for your spiritual development, whether you're on the giving or receiving end of the relationship.

## Overcoming the Pain with Writing Meditation

Another important element of the healing process is changing our attitudes toward other people. It is often difficult to forgive those who have harmed us. If we change the way we feel about people in general, it will be much easier to overcome our anger toward those who have caused us pain. This is where the writing meditation can be instrumental.

By using the loving-kindness writing meditation that I showed you in Step 9, you'll make tremendous progress in transforming the way you feel about others. When you see that they too have wounds in their heart, you'll begin to develop understanding and compassion for their suffering. This will open the door to your heart and allow the mindfulness energy to flow freely, which will make the healing process much easier, and less painful.

I want to share with you a story about a lady I met that was suffering from severe emotional trauma. For the sake of anonymity, I'll call her Jane. She contacted me one day, desperate to find some relief from her suffering. She had been brutally raped during a home invasion about 7 years earlier, and had been unable to overcome the trauma, despite working with psychiatrists and psychologists.

Jane emailed me asking for help. I realized that I was going to put the mindfulness meditation practice to the test. My general suggestions are to practice the writing and sitting meditation daily, and get involved in a meditation group, or some other form of support group. But in her case, I felt she needed a little more. Here's what I suggested to her:

- **Begin sitting meditation daily.** I sent her a complimentary copy of our CD, *Quick Start to Mindfulness Meditation,* to help her get started.

- **Practice loving-kindness writing meditation twice a day,** once in the morning and again in the evening before bed.

- **Get involved in a support group.** This would provide her with the spiritual support she needed.

- **Continue seeking professional help.**

In addition to following these suggestions, Jane read our ebook, *Mastering Relationships with Mindfulness* daily. If you noticed, the only additional suggestion I gave her was to do the writing meditation twice daily, instead of just once.

I was eager to hear how the practice was working for her. About two weeks later, Jane emailed me an enthusiastic thank you note. She said, "The difference is phenomenal. My attitude is changing along with having overcome spiritual blockages." She added that she had also overcome the grief of her husband's death from cancer. She said that several people had noticed a difference in her.

> A retreat has the power to heal just about any wound from your past.

I was so happy to hear that Jane was finally getting some relief from her suffering. Her breakthrough reaffirmed my faith in the mindfulness meditation practice, especially the writing meditation. By changing the way we feel about people who have harmed us, we allow the healing process to take place, and this is exactly what the loving-kindness writing meditation does.

## The Healing Power of a Retreat

A mindfulness meditation retreat is the most effective tool for healing the wounds from the past, because it employs the full power of all Three Jewels—the Buddha, the Dharma, and the Sangha.

A retreat has the power to heal just about any wound from your past. I've even seen people overcome painful experiences from the horrors of war. I believe the most effective retreat will be grounded in the basics of a mindfulness meditation practice. The right retreat contains the most important elements of the healing process: instruction from an experienced teacher, plenty of time for meditation, and a supportive environment.

Ideally, you'd want a mindfulness meditation retreat that specifically focuses on healing, though these may be hard to find. The retreat would be designed to walk you through the healing process, and provide you with the necessary spiritual support.

## Conclusion

The reason many people have difficulty overcoming their pain and suffering is because they only examine their problems in an attempt to gain greater understanding. While this is necessary, it is not sufficient. The practice of mindfulness meditation involves understanding our problems, and developing the inner strength to overcome them.

> *"Difficulties are meant to rouse, not discourage. The human spirit is to grow strong by conflict."*
>
> ~ WILLIAM ELLERY CHANNING

The healing process I've outlined in this step may sound simplistic, but I can assure you that it really works, and fast. By developing inner strength, we can heal just about any wound in our heart. I've seen people overcome the traumas of sexual abuse, violence, and war in a fairly short period of time. This approach has worked for millions of people for over 2,500 years—and it will certainly work for you, no matter how long you've struggled with painful memories.

It takes courage and determination to confront the wounds from your past, but it is essential if you want to keep growing and find freedom from your pain and suffering. It may seem like a daunting task, but it's much easier with the support of a sangha. If you practice mindfulness meditation diligently, you will become strong enough to confront any unpleasant memory. You will overcome the wounds from your past once and for all.

Many of us can justifiably blame other people in our past for the wounds in our heart. While others may have indeed caused us harm, it is impractical to expect them to repair the damage done. Therefore, it becomes our responsibility to put ourselves back together. We can and should seek the help of others, but we are each ultimately responsible for our own well-being. Others can walk this spiritual path with us, but not for us.

With everything you've learned so far about mindfulness meditation, you've gained a solid foundation of the practice. It is now time to help carry the message to others. By living mindfully, you will be an example of unconditional love and peace. Your life will be your message, and thus, your words and actions will have a much greater impact.

## Exercises

The following exercises will help you overcome the wounds from your past. They generally revolve around dwelling in the Three Jewels—your sources of mindfulness energy. In particular, the sangha and the mindfulness meditation retreat will be the most effective in healing, with the least amount of effort and pain.

**1. Practice writing meditation.** Go to our website (http://www.Mindfulness Meditation Institute.org) and download a printable copy of the loving-kindness writing meditation. Follow the instructions provided. If you're suffering from severe emotional trauma, I suggest doing the writing meditation twice a day; once in the morning, and again in the evening before bed. If you practice both the sitting and writing meditation daily, you will see noticeable progress in healing the wounds from your past.

**2.  Investigate unresolved issues further.** When painful memories arise during your meditation, investigate them further. Use your developing concentration, mindfulness, and wisdom to look at those memories more objectively. Examine the reasons why you feel hurt. Also, try to see how those who have harmed you were suffering themselves.

Write your observations in your meditation journal. This will help you see them more clearly. Do not stray far from practicing concentration and mindfulness during your meditation sessions, as these are essential to the healing process.

**3.  Get involved in a sangha that will support you in your mindfulness meditation practice.** If there are none in your area, you can start one. Remember, all it takes is two people to start a sangha. Refer to Step 7 for starting a sangha, and Step 12 for sangha-building. To make things easier, you can also download a free mindfulness meditation group starter kit from our website.

**4.  Find a guide or mentor.** It isn't necessary that they have a tremendous amount of experience. The main purpose is to have someone you can confide in, and who can help you apply the practice to your daily life. The relationship works both ways. You'll also be helping him with his spiritual development, so don't be shy about asking someone. He'll likely be honored by your request.

**5.  Mindfulness meditation retreat.** If at all possible, attend a mindfulness meditation retreat, preferably one that specifically focuses on the healing process. This will give you the strength and support you need to heal the wounds from your past as quickly as possible.

# STEP 12

## Transform Your Life and the World through Mindful Living

*If you think in terms of a year, plant a seed; if in terms of 10 years, plant trees; if in terms of 100 years, teach the people.*

~ CONFUCIUS

### Chapter Highlights

- Sharing the Gift: The Culmination of Your Practice
- How to Build a Strong and Healthy Sangha
- Living a Mindful Life for Peace and Harmony
- Mindful Consumption of the Enlightened Person
- Mindfulness and the Evolution of Systems
- Conclusion
- Exercises

**Step 12** *"Having found freedom from our suffering through mindfulness meditation, we shared this practice with others, and continued dwelling deeply in the present moment through mindful living."*

WHEN I BEGAN MY SPIRITUAL JOURNEY, I was a troubled young man. I had no great expectations of achieving enlightenment. In fact, I didn't even know the meaning of the words spirituality, enlightenment, or meditation. All I wanted was to stop hurting. I wanted to be freed from my own prison.

Now 30 years later, I find myself with a rich and fulfilling life and teaching others how to find freedom from their suffering. It has been a challenging journey at times, but that just makes me appreciate my inner peace even more. I also appreciate all the people who have helped me along my path. They each hold a special place in my heart.

Most of us on a spiritual path want to become more enlightened. That is, we want to expand our awareness. In order to do so, not only do we need to diligently practice mindfulness, but we also need to look beyond our immediate environment. We need to see how our actions affect our family, community, and the rest of the world. If we are not mindful of our interconnectedness, and do not feel a sense of duty to help others, then we are not truly enlightened.

*"A small body of determined spirits fired by an unquenchable faith in their mission can alter the course of history."*

~ MAHATMA GANDHI

If you've put into practice the previous eleven steps, then you have a good understanding of the mindfulness meditation practice, and no doubt you've already seen a significant transformation in yourself and your relationships. You are well on your way to reaching the next level in your spiritual evolution.

Sadly, many people stop short of realizing their full spiritual potential. They settle for a comfortable personal life, and modest level of peace and happiness. While this is certainly desirable if they didn't have these things before, they are missing out on a much greater level of inner peace, and an opportunity to make a significant impact in the world. In addition, their suffering will return as they get older and have to grapple with their own mortality. The only way to put an end to all of our suffering is to keep moving forward on our spiritual path.

In Step 12, you're going to learn how to put your mindfulness into action through mindful living and carrying the message of personal freedom. Not only will these help you continue growing, but they will also help you be of greater service to your community.

Mindful living will enable you to make a significant contribution to the world. As you develop mindfulness, you will gain an awareness of the interdependent nature of your existence, and see how your actions have far-reaching implications in the world. You'll gain an appreciation for the limited resources we need for our survival, and start working toward their preservation, so that we do not put unnecessary stress on our environment and on fragile societies.

Mindful living will also help you set an example for others to follow. People will begin to see you as a leader. They will see that you have the inner strength and conviction to stand up for sound moral principles. You are becoming a pioneer in the next generation of leaders. You are becoming a mindful leader.

You can also make a significant contribution by sharing the practice of mindfulness meditation with others. You will gain an enormous amount of joy and fulfillment from helping them. It is deeply satisfying to see people overcome difficulties they've struggled with their whole lives, and find true inner peace and happiness. Each person will be forever grateful because you will have made a tremendous difference in his life. You truly have a gift to share with the world.

## Sharing the Gift: The Culmination of Your Practice

Now that you've gained enough wisdom and experience to teach mindfulness meditation, it's time to pass it on to others. You have valuable experience that other people want, and need you to share with them.

You don't need to wait years before you begin teaching. I began teaching meditation after only a couple of months of experience. You are now a fully qualified teacher, and a messenger of peace and harmony.

> *"Be a rainbow in someone else's cloud."*
> ~ Maya Angelou

Sharing the practice with others is an essential part of your spiritual development. By not doing it, you will deprive yourself of several elements vital to your spiritual growth:

- **Develop a deeper understanding of the practice.** The wonderful part about teaching others is that you'll also learn a great deal—maybe even more than your students. By teaching others, you will challenge yourself to explain the practice in terms that others can understand.

- **Cultivate more intimate relationships.** The relationships you cultivate will be on a deeper level, and will be great sources of spiritual nourishment. They will enhance your growth significantly.

- **Gain tremendous enjoyment from helping others.** Watching others overcome their suffering is a deeply gratifying and fulfilling experience, and their enthusiasm will motivate them to share the practice with others.

- **Gain a sense of purpose.** Teaching mindfulness meditation, in and of itself, is a great service to your community because you will be helping others find freedom from their suffering. When you share the practice of mindfulness meditation, you cultivate peace, harmony, and goodwill everywhere you go.

Sharing the practice with others is amazingly simple. You can start by telling the people you already know, such as friends, colleagues, and family members. You don't have to be pushy. Remember, you're trying to help them, not convert them. Simply tell them how the practice has transformed you and your relationships, and assure them that they don't have to abandon their spiritual roots to practice mindfulness meditation. In fact, it will help them better understand their current spiritual beliefs. Then simply show them how they can find out more about the practice.

Once people get started in the practice, encourage them to also pass it on to others. This will give them a sense of purpose by making an important contribution to society.

If you're more ambitious, then the possibilities are only limited by your imagination. You can use social media to tell others about mindfulness meditation. If you have an extended network of friends and colleagues, you can pass it on to them. I'm sure by now you've probably told a few people, so you already have a head start. Whatever your situation, you can get creative in carrying the message of peace and harmony. Together we can change the world in ways that political leaders cannot.

## How to Build a Strong and Healthy Sangha

A mindfulness meditation group, or sangha, is vital to your continued spiritual growth. While meditating alone is an important element of your practice, so is meditating with others. The sangha will provide you with the support and spiritual nourishment you need to grow, and help you stay committed to your practice.

*"If you knew what I know about the power of giving, you would not let a single meal pass without sharing it in some way."*

*~ Buddha*

Look for a sangha in your area that is grounded in good mindfulness meditation techniques. If there is none, consider starting one. Starting a sangha is easy, and immensely rewarding. For a discussion about starting a sangha, refer back to Step 7, where we discussed it in detail.

To make things easy for you, I've prepared a group starter kit that provides you with a sample format, a preamble, and some literature about the practice. These will help you stay focused on your primary purpose. You can download it from the Resources section of our website.

## Recruiting New Members Is Essential

If you recall, the whole point of starting a meditation group is to generate more mindfulness energy, which will speed up your spiritual development, and that of others. Therefore, recruiting new members should be a high priority, and an ongoing activity. Remember, because of the rising popularity of mindfulness meditation, there are many people out there looking for your sangha. Help them find you.

Word of mouth is probably the most effective, but there are also many other options. You can put up flyers at your local libraries, health food stores, religious centers, chiropractic offices, and other health care facilities. You can even find an online directory that lists all the different meditation groups in your area. They are usually more than happy to add your group to the list.

Most doctors are happy to pass on information that will help their patients live healthier lives. I told my doctor about this book, and she told many of her patients about it. Helping other people is that simple.

One tactic I've found extremely useful is to list our meeting with the local TV stations. Most of them have a calendar of events for their viewers, and they encourage event organizers to submit their events. There is usually no charge for this. Just go to their website, and search for their calendar of events.

An additional benefit to listing your group with local TV stations is that other publications will sometimes pick up your listing and publish it in their periodical. We've had group members find us through publications that I'd never even heard of.

There are also many other local sites that list events in your area.

Simply do a search on Google for "submit an event + your city" and you'll find many of them. If you list your meeting as a weekly event, it will most likely be on their website indefinitely. This is great for getting exposure.

Those of you who are members of twelve-step fellowships have a huge audience of people interested in meditation. Spread the word among your fellow members, but don't make any announcements during the meetings, as it would be a violation of their Traditions.

Some of the most enthusiastic people I've found are those early in their recovery from alcohol or drug addiction. They are serious about their recovery, and eager to learn anything that will enhance their spiritual development. Some treatment facilities are very receptive to having a meditation meeting that is easily accessible to their clients, so you may want to inquire.

Another group that is interested in meditation is the Unitarian Universalist church. Its members are liberal in their religious views, and like people in recovery, are also interested in things that will enhance their spiritual development. While they are generally receptive to having a meeting at their facility, remember to keep your meeting autonomous, or you could easily lose the focus on your primary purpose.

You can get really creative in recruiting new members. If you're savvy with social media, you can use sites such as Twitter and Facebook to reach people in your area. Remember, there are many people out there just as interested in finding you, as you are in finding them. You'll be doing them a great service by reaching them.

I do want to point out one pitfall that some groups fall into. Sometimes, when a small group reaches a point where the members become very comfortable with each other, they become reluctant to recruit new members because they don't want strangers upsetting the cozy environment. Now the group has become exclusive. When this happens, everyone stops growing. Don't make this mistake. If we close ourselves off to other people, then we miss the whole point of our spiritual development. So keep recruiting new members.

## *Teaching the Practice Is Fundamental*

Ongoing instruction is another important element of a thriving sangha, so I would suggest you incorporate it into your meetings. The good news is that here at the Mindfulness Meditation Institute, we've developed various tools to help you teach the

> If you want to keep progressing, then you must continue learning.

practice. They include this book, guided meditation CDs, a workbook, and retreats. These will make it easy for you to pass it on to others.

Next, you need to decide when to give instruction, because any time spent on instruction is time taken away from meditation. Though this isn't necessarily bad, I think you always want to devote a considerable part of the meeting to actual meditation. After all, isn't meditating with others the whole idea behind starting a sangha? You need to find a good balance between instruction and meditation. Remember, if you want to keep progressing, then you must continue learning.

## *Mentoring Others: One of Your Greatest Learning Tools*

One way to address the ongoing need for instruction is to have group members mentor each other. A mentor, or teacher, can act as a personal guide in the practice of mindfulness meditation. He can give his apprentice guidance through written assignments or practical exercises. This teacher/student relationship can be extremely rewarding for both. Very often, the teacher gets more out of the relationship than the student. And you don't need a lot of experience. In fact, you already have enough experience to be a mentor.

Mentoring other members may not be your preferred area of service work, but you won't find out until you try it. Besides, other people need for you to share your valuable experience. It's wonderful to see someone else find inner peace, and know that you had a part in it. Mentoring will not only keep everyone grounded in the basic principles, but it will also keep everyone motivated and growing, and will enable you to devote more of your meeting time to actual meditation.

## The Importance of Getting Involved

I also recommend that you encourage members to get involved in the sangha. As your sangha grows, there will be various duties that need to be carried out. Have members commit to performing these duties as term commitments. Some examples are:

- **Secretary.** This person would be responsible for setting up the room every week, and finding members to lead the meetings.

- **Recruiter.** This person will lead the new member recruiting efforts. He doesn't have to do all the work himself, but he would coordinate the recruiting campaign.

- **Tea person.** The tea person would be responsible for making tea for the group every week, and maybe helping the secretary set up the meeting.

- **Treasurer.** The treasurer is responsible for managing the funds and paying the bills for the sangha.

- **Group chairperson.** The chairperson would help coordinate the functions of the group, and facilitate the monthly (or bimonthly) business meetings. This is not a position of authority, but rather coordination.

Your sangha will need to raise some funds to pay for its expenses. Probably the best way to do this is through member donations. If you pass a basket sometime during each meeting, members can contribute a dollar, or two. You should make it clear that contributions are voluntary, so nobody feels obligated. This should raise sufficient funds to meet your expenses.

It's also important not to accept funds from outside organizations, or large contributions from any members, as this can imply an obligation of a return favor, and will begin to adversely affect the sangha's focus on its primary purpose.

The important decisions should be made by voting at the business meetings, held maybe once a month or every other month. I recommend that the positions be for terms of six months to a year, with no member serving more than one consecutive term. Regular rotation is important, so that no individuals get the chance to dominate the group. It also gives everyone valuable experience practicing mindfulness when working with others.

## Suggestions to New Members

The following are some ideas I borrowed from different twelve-step programs. They have a formula that works well for keeping members involved in their spiritual development, and in the groups. They make these suggestions to newcomers to keep them on the right track.

For them, it is vital to stay focused on their spiritual development because in the beginning, it's easy to revert to the behavior that got them in so much trouble. They consider the suggestions necessary for staying committed to their spiritual path:

**Attend meetings regularly.** The sangha provides a great deal of support to our practice, but we must be there to avail ourselves of this benefit.

**Find a mentor.** The mentor can provide more in-depth instruction than can be provided at meetings. Furthermore, he can provide support in much the same way as a sangha. Don't worry about feeling like you're bothering him by asking him to devote some of his spare time to helping you, because you're also helping him stay focused and motivated. An enlightened person will be happy to help.

**Practice mindfulness meditation regularly.** Remember that the more you practice, the faster you'll progress. Some people say they're not interested in becoming a guru. That's not the point of the practice. The only time you may be practicing too much is when you begin neglecting your responsibilities, or when you practice simply for your own benefit, and not helping others.

**Be a mentor to others.** Make yourself available to mentor other members. Mindfulness meditation instruction should be part of your regular practice. As you awaken spiritually, you'll begin to see how everyone benefits from helping each other.

**Get involved in recruiting new members.** If your sangha is strong and growing, then everyone will grow faster. This will also give members a stake in the group, and help keep them committed to its success.

**Get members' phone numbers, and use them.** Calling other members helps us stay connected spiritually. Email and texting are fine for quick messages or business purposes, but of low spiritual value because you're usually not communicating in the present moment, and therefore, not making a conscious contact. You can call other members not just to talk about the practice, but also to get to know each other on a more personal level, or maybe just to say hi. Very often, someone might be having a rough day, and simply needs to hear another person's voice.

**Try the practice for two weeks.** Suggest to new members that they meditate for half an hour each day for fourteen days straight using the basic mindfulness meditation techniques. Also ask them to do the writing meditation (Step 9, exercise 3). This combination is pretty effective at convincing them to continue the practice, because they'll see significant changes in themselves in that one week.

If you follow these suggestions, soon your sangha will be growing strong, and members will be making great progress in their practice. In the twelve-step programs, members often make these suggestions around the end of their meetings. I recommend you do the same. It's a formula that has worked very well for them for over 79 years. I've summarized them in The 5 Suggestions of the Mindfulness Meditation Practice, which you can find in the appendix and the group starter kit.

## The Value of Social Activities

I've found socializing to be an invaluable element to the success of the sangha, and to the individual's personal development. Some people view it as nothing more than entertainment. I think differently. Socializing is essentially connecting with other people at some spiritual level, like we discussed in Step 7. You can develop more meaningful relationships with other members, which will enhance your spiritual development. It also helps make your practice much more enjoyable.

When I lived in Miami, our sangha had members specifically responsible for organizing social activities. You don't need a reason for a get-together, but holidays and group anniversaries are good excuses. You may also have regular activities, such as a once-a-month potluck. I would suggest you incorporate the same practice. It will help members feel like they're a part of an important cause. They will also make new friends.

## Keeping Your Sangha Focused Is Vital

Staying focused on your primary purpose is essential to the effectiveness and long-term success of your sangha. It's tempting to get involved in charitable work unrelated to your sangha's core mission. While these intentions are noble, I think it's a mistake because it's a sure way for your sangha to lose its focus—and once this happens, it's almost impossible to get it back.

As I mentioned in Step 7, probably the best way to keep your sangha focused is to read a preamble that outlines your primary purpose at the beginning of every meeting. This will eliminate any confusion, so that the sangha always remains a refuge for anyone needing spiritual support. Remember, the group starter kit from our website provides you with a sample format, preamble, and literature to help you stay focused.

Though I recommend against the sangha getting involved in outside causes, I would encourage you, as an individual, to get involved in any volunteer work you like. Remember that your community is your extended sangha, and you should make a contribution of your time and effort. So get involved in outside projects as much as you like, just don't involve the sangha.

## Living a Mindful Life for Peace and Harmony

Mindful living is another essential element of our spiritual development. Although a discussion of the entire Noble Eightfold Path is beyond the scope of this book, we have already discussed some of them. For now, I want to show you how to practice mindful living. This will not only help you transform your life, but it will also transform your relationships with everyone you encounter. All in all, it will make life a lot more pleasant and enjoyable for you, and those around you.

> *"If we are peaceful, if we are happy, we can smile and blossom like a flower, and everyone in our family, our entire society, will benefit from our peace."*
>
> ~ THICH NHAT HANH

Remember that our suffering is the result of our unmindful reactions to the events in our lives. So our goal is to achieve freedom from suffering by developing mindfulness, which will enable us to understand the true nature of the human condition.

Throughout our whole lives, we've developed views and behaviors that we use to deal with various situations. These are called mental formations. We get very comfortable with our views because we don't have to expend energy thinking about how to handle situations with which we are already familiar. Now, with our emerging mindfulness, we're going to see how well these mental formations are serving us, and how we can handle these situations differently, so that they don't create suffering in our lives, and in the lives of others.

### How Mindfulness Makes You More Productive

I sometimes tell people that they could accomplish so much more in their lives, if they just learned to slow down. This sounds like a paradox, but when I explain it to them, it makes perfect sense.

Remember the story I told you earlier about the man riding the horse? It's worth repeating the story for this discussion. A man was riding his horse quickly down the road. He looked determined about where he was going. A bystander was curious, so he asked him, "Where are you going?" and the man replied, "I don't know. Ask the horse."

> To shorten our path to inner peace, we need to slow down and cultivate a deeper awareness of our goals and actions.

This story is told in Eastern traditions to illustrate what an agitated mind does to us. Very often, we feel compelled to stay busy because we want to feel like we're being productive, or accomplishing something in our lives. We usually do this without having a clear plan of where we're going, or what we're trying to accomplish. Furthermore, our values change as we get older. The things we deemed important when we were younger are not so important today, yet our commitments may not necessarily reflect these changing values.

To make matters worse, we have this nagging feeling that we need to be somewhere else, doing something else. In other words, we're always in a hurry because we subconsciously think that we'll be happier when we arrive at that other place.

By slowing down, we become more focused and mindful of where we're going, so we can determine the most efficient and effective way of getting there. But even more importantly, we become more mindful of whether our original goal will indeed lead to happiness. So in order to shorten our path to inner peace, we need to slow down and cultivate a deeper awareness of our goals and actions.

Calming our mind is not so difficult once we know how. The hard part is remembering to apply our developing concentration and mindfulness to our daily activities. It's easy for us to let our mind drift away, and forget about being in the present moment. The good news is that you'll naturally learn to live in the present moment by continuing to practice mindfulness meditation. One of the first things that we should be mindful of is our practice itself. Remember, as with learning how to play a musical instrument, it's essential to practice regularly and stay grounded in the basics.

Several years ago, I decided I wanted to learn how to sing, so I took private lessons from an opera singer. Like many people who like to sing, I often sang along with the radio as best as I could. When I started taking lessons, I quickly realized that I wasn't using proper techniques. My teacher taught me the necessary techniques, and I had to practice them using scales.

In time, I gained better control over my voice and could sing progressively more difficult songs. However, no matter how much I progressed, I still needed to continue practicing scales to further develop my voice. It wasn't long before I could sing beautiful Italian arias.

My experience with meditation has been the same. I've learned to stay grounded in the basics of practicing concentration and mindfulness. As I become more proficient with these techniques, I'm able to look deeper into other subjects of meditation, such as impermanence, interbeing, and suffering. I know how tempting it is to try new things. That's what I like about the mindfulness meditation practice; there's plenty of room for variety without straying off course.

In Steps 8 and 9, I shared with you some useful tools that will help you in your spiritual development. If you recall, they revolved around practicing mindfulness in your daily activities. We used them as tools to further our personal goals—that is, our own spiritual development. Now we're going to look at them with regard to how they affect the world around us.

As you develop concentration, you'll gain a deeper insight into the implications of your actions. With your developing mindfulness, you'll be able to choose wisely where to direct your concentration. Then you will gain a greater understanding of your relationship with the rest of humanity, and you'll gain the wisdom to promote peace and harmony in the world. Here are some examples:

**Mindful breathing and mindful walking.** By practicing these, you'll become a beacon of peace and serenity. The energy of mindfulness emanating from you will shine onto everyone you encounter, and you will help others achieve freedom from their suffering.

**Deep listening.** This is such a powerful tool for cultivating peace and harmony. So many people suffer from neglect, especially children and the elderly. You can provide them with a tremendous amount of healing energy if you simply take a few minutes to just listen to them. This works especially well with young people who are trying to make sense of their lives. Listening can also go a long way toward helping those with deep wounds in their heart.

**Mindful speech.** Words can create either harmony or disharmony. We usually don't listen to the words that come out of our mouth, in terms of how other people might perceive them. Our speech is often an expression of our emotions. It is a reaction to something that brings us pleasure, or displeasure. Few of us train ourselves to think carefully before we speak. One technique that I've found very useful is to pause before I speak, and then choose words that are healing and nurturing. Another helpful technique is to practice deep listening on myself. By listening to myself, I can get a better sense of what others hear.

**Non-judging and forgiveness.** Judging people harshly is a habit that is deeply ingrained in us. When people do something wrong or inappropriate, we're ready to criticize them, especially if they can't hear us. It is most common when we don't know the wrongdoer personally. This behavior stems from our distrust of strangers. The best remedy I've found for this is the loving-kindness writing meditation. This practice goes a long way toward helping us change our attitudes about people. It helps us become more compassionate and forgiving of others.

## Mindful Consumption of the Enlightened Person

Mindful consumption is one of the most prominent qualities of an enlightened person. It takes wisdom to see the repercussions our consumption has throughout the world. A truly enlightened person is first concerned about how his own actions impact the world. Then he is willing to help others become more mindful, yet he is not attached to the outcomes. He is understanding and forgiving of other people's faults, and works tirelessly to promote mindful consumption.

> Mindful consumption is one of the most prominent qualities of an enlightened person.

When we're attached to a cause, we do good deeds for personal gratification, and we get angry when others don't meet our expectations. For example, many years ago I did volunteer work in the prison system. I was young and wanted to give back to my community, but I also enjoyed the recognition I received from the inmates and my friends. Today, I do volunteer work at the local homeless shelter, but not for the recognition. I do it because I care about the well-being of the people I am helping.

Most of us have practiced mindful consumption at one time or another, usually when there's been a downturn in the economy. During such times, we're forced to be more careful of our spending, especially if we're unemployed. I've certainly had that experience a couple of times in my life. It's much easier to be mindful of our consumption when it affects us directly, but what about when it doesn't? This is where our developing concentration and mindfulness can help.

> We all have the seeds of enlightenment within us. It's just a matter of cultivating them.

As your True Nature awakens, you'll begin to see your interconnectedness with the rest of the world, and how your welfare is tied to the welfare of others. Gradually, your ego will begin to dissipate, as you see past the illusion of a separate self. That is when you will develop a greater concern for others, and contribute to society without personal motives. It takes some work, but if you keep putting forth the right effort, you will certainly get there. We all have the seeds of enlightenment within us. It's just a matter of cultivating them.

## Mindfulness and the Evolution of Systems

In order to see the bigger picture, we need to look for it. Throughout my career, I've studied various subjects involving major social and environmental issues. I've been involved in fields such as business and economics, the natural sciences, anthropology, political science, public administration, and more. This has enabled me to see the bigger picture. I've gained a deep appreciation of how everything is interconnected, and how our individual actions have global implications—especially in our consumption of resources.

> "We are here to awaken from our illusion of separateness."
>
> ~ Thich Nhat Hanh

During my graduate studies at Syracuse University, I developed an interest in a field of study called systems evolution. I gravitated toward it because through my diverse background, I began to see some common patterns in how organizations and societies behaved. I found that there were certain principles by which all systems evolved.

The word system has several different meanings, so it might be a good idea to define the term as it pertains to our discussion. We are talking about systems in a general sense. Basically, a system is a group of components working toward a goal. A living organism is a classic example of a system. Other examples include a city, state, nation, economy, family, and so forth. Everything is part of one system or another. Therefore, everything is interdependent.

Systems evolution is the process by which a system achieves its primary goal(s) in an increasingly more efficient and effective manner. This usually involves increasing levels of complexity and self-awareness in how a system processes inputs to convert them into outputs. In other words, evolution is the increasing mindfulness of a system.

In his book, *Collapse: How Societies Choose to Fail or Succeed*, anthropologist Jared Diamond examined the factors that led to the rise, or decline, of different societies throughout history. He found that the success of a society depended on how well it used its resources. The societies that thrived were mindful of their consumption, and the ones that failed were not.

We often think natural resources are plentiful, and that they'll never run out. We don't normally think about how the oxygen in the air, or the trees might run out because there are so many. However, there have been entire societies that have collapsed because they cut down all their trees. One example is Easter Island. The native people cut down all the trees, and used them as firewood and for other functions in their society. They didn't think they would run out of trees, so they never replenished them. There are numerous other societies where the same thing happened.

The main function of all economies is to make efficient use of its resources to provide desired goods and services for its citizens. In world politics, tensions between nations usually revolve around disputes over resources. One of the most startling statistics I came across when studying international relations between the United States and China was that Americans consume about thirty times more of the world's resources than do the Chinese.

China has more than four times the population of the U.S.; 1.3 billion people versus 300 million, and India has close to 1 billion people. Both China and India have thriving economies where the standards of living are rising quickly. What do you think will happen when all those people begin consuming resources at the same rate as Americans, which is very likely in our lifetime? Consumer prices will rise, and so will tensions between countries. Prices will rise because of the higher demand for consumer products, and the resources needed to produce them. This will be detrimental to fragile societies, as higher food prices will exacerbate the world hunger problem.

The whole point of this discussion is to give you a bigger picture of the world, and some of the trends that will directly affect us in the coming years. Now, the American society is unlikely to collapse any time soon. However, we will certainly see major economic corrections, like the financial crisis of 2008 that led to the demise of several large financial institutions, and almost took the U.S. automakers with them.

Each recession is likely to be more severe than the last one, if we don't become more mindful consumers. Look at how long it has taken us to recover from the recession of 2008. In 2014, job growth was still sluggish, and the economy was growing at a slower than normal pace.

### "Conservation Starts with Me"

Through our normal daily activities, we consume many types of resources. In this section, I will briefly touch on just a few of them to give you some ideas on how you can consume them more mindfully. Remember, they are primarily ways for us to practice mindful consumption—not to impose our views on other people. We can bring about awareness of these issues, but if we try to force our beliefs on others, we will simply alienate them.

Oftentimes, large institutions are inefficient in their use of resources because it takes more bureaucracy to manage them. This raises the cost to the consumer for their products or services. Generally, the larger the market share they have, the more power they have to raise their prices, and the less incentives they have for using resources efficiently.

One way we can help powerful institutions become more efficient is by spending our dollars elsewhere. Competition has a magical way of helping companies become more mindful consumers of resources. It plays an important role in the evolution of a system. It forces the survival of the fittest.

### Eating Mindfully for Developing Awareness

Remember when you were a kid, and your mom told you to eat all your food because there were children starving in Africa? Her point was that you didn't waste any food. Well, she was right. But even mom may not have been fully aware of the gravity of the problem. Every year, tens of millions of children throughout the world die of starvation and malnutrition. Solving the world hunger problem isn't easy, but we certainly can do our part to contribute to the solution, instead of the problem. It starts with us eating more mindfully.

> Solving the world hunger problem starts with us eating more mindfully.

One thing I realized in my own eating habits was that I was eating more than I needed for good health. Today, I try to eat in moderation. I also try to avoid letting food spoil. I often bought more food than I could consume before it spoiled, and ended up throwing away a considerable amount. I am much more careful now. If we could all be more mindful of our consumption of food, we would drive down the prices, and make it more affordable to people living in poverty.

There are other ways to be mindful of our consumption of food. When we eat, we're often in a hurry, so we chew and swallow our food as quickly as possible. There is so much to see in our food, but we never see it because we don't look. For example:

- Is the food we're eating truly nourishing, or is it causing us harm?

- Who dedicated the time and effort in cultivating our food?

- Who dedicated the time and effort in preparing our food?

- How is our consumption of food affecting the planet? The production of food also consumes a significant amount of energy.

Now that our mindfulness is developing, we can see these things if we look closer. Once we see how our consumption of food affects the rest of the world, we can begin to make more mindful choices.

## Mindful Consumption of Energy

Energy use has become a major issue worldwide in recent years. The main reason is that it's beginning to have a greater impact on our daily lives, mainly due to the rising cost of gasoline at the pump. Another reason is that the world is becoming more aware of the environmental impact of the use of petroleum products—that is, global warming. You don't have to be a scientist to see that exhaust fumes from our automobiles are not good for us, or the environment. After all, don't people use the exhaust from their cars to commit suicide?

There are many things we can do to reduce our consumption of energy. I don't want to get into a long discussion, because there is too much to cover on this point. However, we can do things such as change our driving habits, and move toward owning more efficient vehicles and homes. Basically, we want to develop an awareness of how our personal actions affect the environment, and begin changing our energy consumption habits so that we can be an example for others to follow.

## Natural Resources Are Limited

According to the United Nations, the net loss of the world's forests is about 18 million acres each year. That is more than the total acreage in the state of West Virginia—lost every year. Remember from your grade school science class that trees convert carbon dioxide into oxygen, which we need to breathe. Carbon dioxide is also a greenhouse gas, which prevents the heat from the sun from radiating back into space, therefore, contributing to global warming.

In our earlier discussion of systems evolution, I mentioned how deforestation has been a major contributor to the collapse of different societies throughout history. Though the U.S. is not likely to collapse because of deforestation, we are certainly contributing to the demise of other societies that are closer to the edge.

The use of paper products is an area where we can make significant progress toward conservation. I usually cringe when I'm in a public restroom, and I see someone use three or four paper towels to dry his hands, when just one is sufficient. In fact, I often don't even use one paper towel and simply shake off the water, and let my hands dry by themselves. It usually takes only about a minute or so.

Another way to conserve paper is to recycle, and I'm sure you can use your mindfulness to come up with many other ways to conserve trees. Again, mindful consumption needs to start with us, and we shouldn't try to impose our views on other people. If we're arrogant and self-righteous, we'll simply encounter resistance. We can help bring about awareness without being unnecessarily confrontational. This is where mindful speech is invaluable.

In this section, I mentioned just a few ways we can practice mindful consumption, because our actions have far-reaching implications. We do not exist independently of other people and the environment. We depend on others to grow and produce the food we need for our nourishment, and we depend on the environment for such things as clean air and water.

Our actions can either help or harm our environment. If we destroy its ability to provide the things we need for survival, then we hurt ourselves and future generations. By using our developing mindfulness, we can see the effects of our actions and become more responsible partners with our environment, and help others develop the same awareness.

## Conclusion

In Step 12, you learned how to put the mindfulness meditation practice to work to not only transform your life, but also your community. You are now a messenger of peace and harmony, and have the experience and wisdom to teach the practice to other spiritual seekers. By passing it onto others, you are making an important contribution to your community, and playing a vital role in bringing true peace and harmony to our society.

You also learned about mindful consumption. The world is

composed of a wide range of systems that are all interdependent and evolving. We all depend on resources from the environment and other people for our existence. This is why it's so important to cultivate an awareness of the far-reaching implications of our actions. If we want to ensure the survival and evolution of the human race, we need to practice mindful consumption of limited resources, so that we don't stress the world systems to their breaking point.

> *"Never doubt that a small group of thoughtful committed citizens can change the world."*
>
> ~ MARGARET MEAD

Mindfulness is the evolution of human consciousness, and is essential for the long-term survival of the human race. It is a natural progression of our species. As we evolve, we will become more aware of our interdependent nature, and will change our behavior accordingly. The mindfulness meditation practice will help accelerate this process.

You are becoming an enlightened leader, and with enlightenment comes the duty to help others achieve freedom from their suffering, and to promote world peace. You can do this by teaching others the practice of mindfulness, and promoting mindful consumption. You have great talents to share with mankind, and now the world needs you to help build a more mindful society.

## Exercises

Now that you have the wisdom and experience to teach mindfulness meditation, it's important to put it into action to help other people. You can do this by teaching others the practice, and working toward practicing mindful consumption of limited resources. But to have the greatest impact in the world, you must first remain diligent in your own practice.

### Re-examine Your Goals

Now that you have a greater understanding of the practice, it's a good idea to revise your goal statement to incorporate the tools you've learned to use. I suggest including goals for your personal practice, and to help others learn the practice. Depending on your time commitments and interests, you can find different ways of carrying the message. You can get some ideas from the section "Sharing the Gift: The Culmination of Your Practice" at the beginning of this chapter.

Once you have written your new goal statement, I suggest posting it some place where you will see it every day, such as your mirror. This will serve as a reminder of what you're trying to accomplish, so you can stay focused and committed.

## Writing Meditation

Take the living the mindfulness meditation practice writing meditation and write it out by hand for about 10-15 minutes a day. You can find a copy of the meditation in the appendix, and a printable version on our website. This exercise will help you incorporate the practice into your life by making the process natural and effortless. It will help you live the ideals you are striving toward.

I suggest making this writing meditation an ongoing part of your daily routine until the mindfulness meditation practice becomes a way of life. If you ever find yourself drifting off course, you can use it to help you get back on track.

## Mindful Living

**1. Stay focused on the basics of mindfulness meditation** by continuing to develop concentration and mindfulness. This will help you see the implications of your daily activities on a deeper level.

**2. Cultivate peace and harmony in the world around you.** Use mindful breathing, mindful walking, deep listening, mindful speech, and forgiveness and compassion to help bring about healing and transformation in the lives of people around you. Loving-kindness writing meditation will make this effortless. Your inner peace is a powerful example for others to follow.

**3. Examine the far-reaching implications of your daily activities.**
We all depend on other people and the environment for our survival. In
turn, they also depend on us. Use your wisdom to examine how your
actions affect them. Pick an activity, such as your job, and write in your
journal about all those you think are affected by your actions, and how.

**4. Become a more mindful consumer of resources.** We all consume
resources that have their limits. Just about all our activities involve the
consumption of some form of natural resource, such as food, air, water,
plants, minerals, and energy. Strive to consume them in an increasingly
efficient manner, as the exhaustion of limited resources creates social,
economic, and political tensions within and among societies. Maybe
you can use fewer paper products, drive more efficiently, consume fewer
calories, or avoid wasting food.

## Sangha-Building

**1. Get involved in a sangha.** Using the suggestions in Step 12, you
can build a strong and healthy sangha that will be a refuge for you and
others in order to advance your spiritual development. You can do this by
taking on a service commitment in your sangha and/or teaching mindfulness meditation to less experienced members. Choose any function
that suits you and your schedule. The important thing is to get involved.

**2. Help recruit new members.** We should all perform this function
to some degree because it will help keep our sangha healthy and strong.
Recruiting is easy because there are so many people who are interested
in learning how to meditate. One simple and effective approach is to
mention to other people in conversation how you're practicing mindfulness meditation and the benefits you've gained. If they express an interest,
invite them to visit your sangha. If you are more ambitious, you can find
many creative ways to get the word out, such as social media, craigslist,
and event calendars with local TV stations.

**3. Become a mentor.** Newer members need your valuable experience and wisdom to help them with their practice. Let them know that you're available for one-on-one guidance, and show them how to get involved. This is a very rewarding experience for both the student and the teacher, and it doesn't require much of your time. Mentoring usually involves a couple of phone conversations each week, and maybe meeting with your protégé occasionally to discuss and review exercises.

# STAYING THE COURSE

*Energy and persistence conquer all things.*

~ BENJAMIN FRANKLIN

## Chapter Highlights

- How We Get Distracted
- Why We Lose Motivation
- How to Get Back on Track
- Take Your Spiritual Growth to New Heights
- You Now Have the Tools to Succeed
- Recipe for Success
- How a Mindfulness Meditation Retreat Will Keep You on Track
- What's Next?
- Conclusion
- Exercises

CONGRATULATIONS! YOU'VE MADE IT through all 12 Steps. I admire your dedication and commitment. I'm sure that by now you've changed in many ways. You are probably more peaceful, emotionally stable, and are more concerned about the well-being of other people. And certainly, you are more wise and enlightened. While these are great accomplishments, there are still some challenges on the road ahead.

As you've probably noticed, my personal experience with meditation has been challenging at times. I wish I could tell you that I am always diligent and committed to my practice. But the truth is that I sometimes miss a few days, or get temporarily sidetracked. Unexpected events come up in my life that divert my attention, and I soon find myself getting off my meditation routine. So, don't feel bad if this happens to you.

As masters have pointed out, the only thing that is constant is change. Much of our suffering arises from our belief that when we get all the things we want, we'll live happily ever after. Though most of us realize that this is just a fantasy, we often cling to the things that bring us pleasure.

We all experience significant changes in our lives. We may get a promotion at work, start a new family, or encounter an illness in the family. All of these can force us to prioritize our activities and rearrange our schedules. Change is unavoidable.

We are most susceptible to getting off track in our meditation practice during times of change. Until we are totally convinced that our practice will improve every area of our lives, we will always remain willing to sacrifice it for something more important to us.

Certainly, life and death situations are more urgent than meditation. But for the most part, if we give up our practice when we experience changes in our lives, we will likely make things more difficult for ourselves. The stress of a new job, family, or illness can become intolerable if we are not getting spiritual strength from our practice. Our pain and suffering will return.

In this chapter, I will go over some of the reasons why we get sidetracked in our meditation practice. I will then give you some suggestions for getting back on track, for when you do get sidetracked by unavoidable circumstances. I will also share with you some tools for helping you stay motivated and committed to your practice.

It is important to remain diligent with your practice if you want to continue growing. Otherwise, you will revert to old thinking and behavior, which will bring back the pain and suffering you worked so hard to overcome.

## How We Get Distracted

With all your activities and personal commitments, it's easy to get sidetracked when you encounter changes in your life. Distractions can easily derail your efforts when you're early in your meditation practice, causing you to lose your hard-earned spiritual growth. Here are some of the most common ways of getting off track:

**Traveling.** When traveling, we get off our routine and get involved in different activities away from our regular place of meditation. This makes it difficult to find a quiet time and place for sitting meditation.

**Unexpected changes.** Sometimes, things in our life can change without warning. We experience tragedies or circumstances beyond our control that force us to make drastic changes in our lives. In such situations, one of the first things we drop is our meditation practice, because doing so doesn't usually put us in imminent danger.

**Looking for greener pastures.** Many of us get sidetracked by experimenting with different forms of meditation. It's tempting to try a new form of meditation when a friend raves about one that made him feel great. There is nothing inherently wrong with other forms. After all, mindfulness meditation isn't the only right way to achieve inner peace. The problem arises when you start jumping from one form of meditation to another without a clear understanding of why. If you do this, your progress will slow to a crawl, and you'll begin to see little reason for meditating, and eventually quit altogether.

**Drifting off course.** In the beginning, it's easy to forget to use proper meditation techniques. Next thing you know, you're just going through the motions. When this happens, your progress will suffer, and you'll begin cutting back on your meditation.

In the early stages of your practice, it's easy to get distracted. Once you get off track, you'll slowly lose what you've gained from all your hard work, and you'll have a hard time getting back into your meditation routine. That's why it's much easier to stay focused and committed, so you don't have to go through the struggle of starting up again. One of the ways of staying focused is to remain vigilant of the things that can derail your practice.

## Why We Lose Motivation

Experienced practitioners don't have much of a problem staying motivated and committed to their meditation practice. But for beginners, this is much harder when circumstances change in their lives. Here are the main reasons:

**Lack of progress.** If you follow the techniques I've outlined in the 12 Steps, you'll certainly make noticeable progress in your spiritual development. The problem that some people encounter is that they don't dedicate enough time to their meditation sessions. When you stop seeing progress, you'll lose your motivation and give up, or look for another form of meditation that seems easier.

**Meditation is not yet part of your regular routine.** If we have not yet made it a habit to practice daily, it's easy to get distracted when we're busy or tired. Sometimes we simply forget until it's too late in the day. Then the next day something else happens, and we skip another meditation session. Next thing we know, a whole week has gone by and we start feeling guilty, and to get rid of the guilt we try to forget about meditation altogether.

**Lack of focus, and developing bad habits.** Remember that you're learning a new skill, which involves repeated practice using proper techniques. Over time, our recollection of the instructions begins to fade. When this happens, we begin to develop habits that yield little results, and you know what happens when you stop seeing results.

**Not using the tools.** Using the tools in the 12 Steps requires doing things differently. For example, deep listening requires us to pay close attention when someone is talking to us. It's easy to revert back to our old ways of interacting with other people by getting lost in our thoughts, or trying to pay attention to other things going on at the same time.

**Lack of guidance from a mentor.** Many of us prefer studying alone, but learning mindfulness meditation on our own can be challenging. The role of a mentor is to guide you in the practice. He can teach you how to apply the proper techniques, answer any questions, and alert you when you're going astray. And just as important, he can provide you with the spiritual support you need to help you stay motivated and committed to your practice.

**Lack of commitment to others.** When we practice by ourselves, we have commitments to no-one, and we're not accountable in any way. If we're not involved in a sangha, then we don't have an anchor to keep us from going astray, and we're certainly not receiving the support vital to our development.

Most other forms of meditation instruction don't coach you on how to stay motivated and committed to your practice. They usually assume that you will always see the wisdom in the practice, without an appreciation of how hard it can be in the beginning. No wonder so many people give up after a short period of time.

## How to Get Back on Track

I know how hard it can be to start meditating again once you get distracted. Here are some suggestions I think will help. If it has been a relatively short period of time since you last

> *"Fall seven times. Stand up eight."*
> ~ JAPANESE PROVERB

meditated, the first group of suggestions should get you back in the routine quickly. If you have gone several months without meditating, then also try the second group. They will help you renew your commitment to improving your life.

**Short break:**

- **Do the loving-kindness writing meditation.** This is a great motivational tool, and it will help make your restart as effortless as possible.

- **Begin meditating in short sessions.** Then gradually increase the duration. It is easier to restart your practice with short meditation sessions than to go back to where you left off. You'll get back to your previous level in no time.

- **Do walking meditation.** This is one of the best tools for easing back into your routine, especially if you get too agitated from all your other activities.

- **Call a member of your sangha.** Another member can share his experience, and give you encouragement and support.

**Long break:**

- **Go back to your sangha.** Meditating with others is always motivating. Remember, your spiritual community is there to lend you support when you need it.

- **Revise your goal statement.** Consider if your goals may be overly ambitious. Establish goals that are challenging, yet realistically achievable considering your other commitments. This will help you renew your commitment to your practice.

- **Begin reading this book again.** This will renew your motivation, and refresh your memory of the techniques and tools of your practice. In fact, I suggest reviewing this book regularly even if you haven't gotten sidetracked, as it will help you improve your application of the techniques. Remember, this is your handbook for the mindfulness meditation practice.

> Remember, this is your handbook for the mindfulness meditation practice.

Once you apply these suggestions, you'll see how easy it is to get back into your meditation routine, and continue making progress in your spiritual development. Your enthusiasm may not be as strong as when you started, but your determination and commitment will become stronger as you gain more experience with the practice.

## Take Your Spiritual Growth to New Heights

Do you remember why you started practicing mindfulness meditation in the first place? You had probably heard all the talk about the benefits of the practice, so your curiosity led you to give it a try. In recent years, the scientific community has conducted extensive research to determine the benefits of mindfulness meditation. Here is a small reminder of some of the mental and emotional benefits you will realize when you stay committed to your practice:

**You will develop greater self-confidence.** As fear in you subsides and you develop greater self-awareness, you'll gain more confidence in your abilities. You'll feel much better about yourself, and at ease in social situations. You'll be able to accomplish just about anything you set your mind to, whether it be a career or personal goal.

**Anger will dissipate tremendously.** People will no longer be able to push your buttons because of your inner strength and confidence. With less anger, you'll make better decisions, be free of stress and anxiety, have less conflict in your life, and your relationships will certainly improve.

**Painful memories will no longer haunt you.** As the wounds from your past heal, the memories will stop triggering painful emotions. You will finally be free of them for good.

**Relationships with loved ones will improve** because you'll know how to make deeper spiritual connections with them. You'll be surprised at how the loving-kindness writing meditation alone will transform your relationships. Some of them won't improve, but at least you'll be able to accept them as they are.

**Your mental abilities will improve.** As you gain more control over your mind and eliminate unnecessary thinking, your mind will function more efficiently. You will see improved memory, faster mental processing, greater abstract thinking, and even greater creativity, leading to better decision-making. Imagine the impact this will have on your career and personal life.

**Feelings of loneliness will disappear** because you'll be able to connect with people in a more meaningful way, no matter how shy you may be, or whether or not you're in an intimate relationship.

Probably the most profound effect from your mindfulness meditation practice is a deeper connection with the rest of humanity. As a result, you'll develop much greater compassion and concern for the well-being of others. And your reward will be an inner peace that you never imagined possible.

## You Now Have the Tools to Succeed

You now have the tools to make great strides in your spiritual development. The 12 Steps of the Mindfulness Meditation Practice give you a solid foundation for your practice in an easy-to-follow format. You have this book as your guide, the workbook, CDs to help you. I never had these things when I was learning the practice. Even though I had teachers along the way, most didn't fully understand how to meditate. We all just assumed that meditation was simply about sitting quietly and relaxing.

Learning how to meditate was a slow process for me. Many of the people I knew saw little results from their practice. They were content with mediocre results, but I wasn't. It wasn't until I learned how to apply the mindfulness meditation techniques that my spiritual development really began to take off.

In 1996, I had a profound spiritual awakening. Conditions were just right for me to get a glimpse of nirvana. From that experience, I realized there was a much higher level of spirituality to be achieved, but I wasn't sure what those conditions were. Now that I have a greater understanding of the spiritual principles, I can apply the mindfulness meditation techniques to help me get back there, but more importantly, I can pass it on to you, so you too can achieve the same freedom I have.

## Recipe for Success

So how do you stay on track in your mindfulness meditation practice? Here's a surefire way to staying motivated and committed to your practice:

### Writing Meditation: Your Powerful Ally

In the short-run, writing meditation is probably the most effective tool for keeping you focused on the practice, especially if you include your goal statement as part of the exercise. It will serve as a constant reminder of your goals, and the ideals you are striving for. It's simple and takes very little time. Writing meditation is ideal for when you're traveling, because you can do it just about anywhere you can write, and you don't necessarily need a quiet environment.

What I would suggest is making writing meditation a part of your routine. When traveling, I recommend using the Step 12 writing meditation, living the mindfulness meditation practice. If you absolutely cannot do sitting meditation when you're away from home, this writing meditation will keep you motivated and eager to get back into your meditation routine when you return home.

## Keep Studying and Applying the 12 Steps

One of the distractions I mentioned above was trying all different kinds of meditation. It may sound like a good idea, but it will slow your progress tremendously. What I recommend is that you stay with mindfulness meditation until you have a firm understanding of what meditation is all about. Later, if you decide that you want to explore other traditions, by all means do so until you find a form that is suitable for you. Then commit yourself to that form and practice it diligently.

> As long as you keep using proper techniques, you'll keep progressing.

What I like about mindfulness meditation is that there's plenty of room for variety. As long as you keep using proper techniques, you'll keep progressing. Keep studying and applying these 12 Steps and you'll soon have a good grasp of the techniques. I think that if you practice regularly and keep a journal to set goals and track your progress, then you'll keep moving forward at a brisk pace.

I've mentioned it several times before, and I'll mention it again, for good reasons: remember to keep practicing concentration and mindfulness during your meditation sessions. Developing these observation skills is the core of your practice. You can always improve your proficiency with them, so you never outgrow them. As you develop them further, you'll be able to see reality on a deeper level. It is like a pianist who continues practicing scales in order to develop greater agility with his fingers, enabling him to play more complex pieces of music with ease and grace.

### Get Involved in a Sangha

Active participation in a sangha is one of the most effective ways of staying grounded in your meditation practice, especially if you take on a commitment. This will make you accountable to others, because they will be depending on you. There are many different tasks that need to be performed, and you can choose one that best fits your time schedule and personal preference. You can lead the meditation sessions, give instruction, mentor newer members, or recruit new members. Remember that the sangha is one of the Three Jewels, and it's essential for your spiritual development.

### When Traveling...

If you're unable to do sitting meditation when you're traveling, I would suggest you incorporate mindful breathing and walking into your activities, in addition to the writing meditation. In fact, you can turn any activity into a meditation session if you perform it with concentration or mindfulness. After all, isn't that our objective at home? Now's your chance to put into practice what you've learned in your meditation sessions.

One trick I learned when traveling, or when my schedule is thrown off, is to meditate during idle times, such as waiting at the airport or for an appointment. Very often, I have to wait for twenty minutes or longer. So I simply close my eyes and follow my breathing mindfully. I am able to meditate even if there are other people and distractions in the room. If I just accept the fact that there are distractions, then they don't bother me.

Traveling also offers a great opportunity for connecting with other people and practicing your social skills, as you learned in Step 7. Another powerful technique is connecting with their True Nature without necessarily engaging them in conversation. This works especially well in large gatherings, where there's a tremendous amount of mindfulness energy available. All you have to do is tune into it.

If you have some free time during your trip, why not check out the local sangha? I often look for one before I go on my trip, and make plans to attend. It's a great way to meet and exchange ideas with people who are on the same path as yourself.

> Our practice will help us deal with our emotions, and our sangha will provide us with the spiritual and emotional support we need during times of crisis.

When you return home, get right back into your regular meditation routine. If you wait a few days, then it becomes increasingly harder, because it's easy to just blow it off and get involved in other activities.

## When Things Change in Your Life...

All of us encounter tragedies and other life-changing events at one time or another. Some of us tend to withdraw from social activities, which is understandable. We certainly need some time for ourselves to heal. However, too much isolation will make our situation worse. We need our meditation practice and sangha to help us heal, and make sense of our situation. Our practice will help us deal with our emotions, and our sangha will provide us with the spiritual and emotional support we need during times of crisis.

So when you're going through a difficult time in your life, take refuge in your sangha. That's what it's for. It will help ease the pain, and remind you that you're not alone. It will also speed up the healing process significantly.

## Sharing the Gift of Mindfulness Meditation

A growing sense of duty to help other people is one of the clearest indicators of your spiritual awakening. As your True Nature awakens, you'll begin to see the suffering in other people, and your compassion for them will grow. Furthermore, you'll see how we're all interconnected, and that your well-being is tied to that of others. As you become aware of these things, you'll want to help them find inner peace the same way you have.

Sharing your experience with others is an effective way of staying focused and committed to your practice. Very often in a teacher/student relationship, it is the teacher who benefits the most, because by explaining the practice to others, he is forced to organize the concepts in his own mind.

Furthermore, we're forced to stay at least one step ahead of our students, so we're more inclined to keep learning. And if these aren't reasons enough, there is a great satisfaction in knowing that you've helped someone transform his life. Then that person will become another source of mindfulness energy that will further your spiritual development.

Now that you're becoming enlightened, it's time to pass the gift on to others. Since many people today are experimenting with meditation, they have little understanding of the practice. They need your experience and guidance, and you now know enough to help them get started. These people are looking for you. Help them find you.

Spreading the word is a lot easier than you think. You don't have to be a great public speaker. You can simply share with other people your own experience with the practice, and if they seem interested, send them information and invite them to your meditation group. It's that simple, and you can take great satisfaction in knowing you're changing someone's life for the better. Try it with friends and family members. They'll most likely be very appreciative.

Each of us has his own particular way of helping others. Some like mentoring people, others prefer growing their sangha, and others prefer spreading the word through the Internet. It all depends on our individual skills and preferences. The good news is that we can work together. With the tools available from the Mindfulness Meditation Institute, we can reach many people.

## How a Mindfulness Meditation Retreat Will Keep You on Track

By far, the most effective tool for helping you stay on track is the mindfulness meditation retreat. A retreat will have such a profound impact on your spiritual development that it will eliminate any doubt about the benefits of meditation, therefore, solidifying your commitment to your practice.

I recommend attending at least a 5-7 day retreat, because it takes a couple of days just to unwind. Then the transformation begins. You can make years' worth of progress in your spiritual growth, because your entire time will be devoted to your practice, and it will be free of all the distractions in your life.

> By far, the most effective tool for helping you stay on track is the mindfulness meditation retreat.

I can usually tell which are the people who attend meditation retreats regularly. They are much more advanced in their development than other spiritual seekers. They are more loving, kind, and have an inner peace and strength that most people don't have, and they are truly committed to their meditation practice. A retreat will help you stay committed because you'll meet people like you, with the same goals of achieving freedom from suffering, and who will support you in your practice.

The only problem is that the availability of mindfulness meditation retreats is quite limited. This is because there are millions of people like you who are interested in learning the practice, but not enough teachers. According to the National Institute of Health, in 2007 there were 20 million people in the United States who had tried meditation, compared to 15 million in 2004. In 2014, that figure was probably around 25 million. With all these people wanting to learn how to meditate, mindfulness meditation retreats are in short supply. Here at the Mindfulness Meditation Institute we're working on doing something about this problem. We're trying to make mindfulness meditation retreats more accessible.

## What's Next?

Now that you've put the 12 Steps into practice, I'm sure you're wondering what comes next. Once you have developed some level of proficiency with concentration and mindfulness, you'll be ready for a more advanced level of mindfulness meditation practice. In an upcoming book, I'll teach you about the Four Establishments of Mindfulness: the body, feelings, the mind, and phenomena. This will help you understand yourself on a deeper level.

At this level, you'll be able to explore more complex subjects such as interbeing, impermanence, and the absence of a separate self. These principles have important implications toward our relationship with the rest of humanity and our mortality. I will guide you through this process in a future book.

In an upcoming book on relationships, you'll learn about the principles that govern all our interactions with other people, whether they are intimate relationships, or casual interactions. You will learn how to apply the practice to your relationships with other people. Though I've already shared with you some tools you can apply to relationships, I've only scratched the surface.

You will also learn how to use these principles to disengage from the power struggles that pervade most of our interactions. The result will be a life that is, for the most part, free of interpersonal conflicts. Though there will still be disagreements with other people, your feelings will no longer be hurt.

At the advanced level of the practice, you'll see an extinguishment of the ego, and all its insecurities. As a result, you'll no longer need validation, and you'll have a much greater sense of who you really are. Fear will continue to dissipate, and you'll stop worrying about your needs being met. You will become proactive, instead of reactive.

You will become one of a few people who have a deep desire to take his spiritual evolution to a much higher level. You'll become a leader among people, and gain a sincere concern for the well-being of others.

This will enable you to make deeper spiritual connections with them, which will help you grow even faster. The whole nature of your existence will be transformed, and you will know true inner peace.

## Conclusion

Starting a meditation practice is easy, but staying focused and committed can be more of a challenge, especially in the beginning. Things are always changing in our lives, and these changes can distract us from our meditation routine, and these are often the times when we need our practice the most. Our meditation practice will help us navigate through stressful situations with calm emotions and a clear mind.

> *"Always bear in mind that your own resolution to succeed is more important than any one thing."*
>
> ~ ABRAHAM LINCOLN

In this chapter, I gave you some suggestions for getting back into your meditation routine when you've been temporarily distracted. Whether it's been a week or two since you last meditated, or several months, these suggestions will help you ease back into your routine relatively quickly.

I also shared with you various tools for staying engaged in your meditation practice. They all revolve around goals and commitments. It may take a bit more effort to stay focused in the beginning of your practice. However, as you gain some experience, not only will you reap the rewards of your efforts, but the practice will become a way of life.

How far you take your spiritual development is entirely up to you. Your progress will depend on how much you practice, and how well you apply the techniques. Remember, until we have reached full enlightenment, there is always the potential for more growth, and an ever-increasing level of peace and serenity.

I heard an expression one day early on my spiritual journey. A speaker was talking about staying committed to a spiritual practice. He said, "It's harder to fall off the edge, if you're standing in the middle." His point really hit home with me. Since then, I have remained involved in my spiritual practice and teaching others, and my life has been transformed beyond my wildest dreams. It can happen to you too. The mindfulness meditation practice will transform the life of anyone who remains diligent and committed to it.

## Exercises

Here are some suggestions for helping you stay committed to your meditation practice. They are designed to keep you connected to the Three Jewels, your sources of spiritual nourishment. If you follow these suggestions, I can assure you that you won't have any trouble staying focused and committed to your meditation practice, and will continue growing.

**1. Practice writing meditation regularly.** Use the Step 12 writing meditation, living the mindfulness meditation practice to help you stay focused on your practice. Remember to include your revised goal statement as part of the exercise. Ideally, you would want to do writing meditation daily for 10-15 minutes. If you cannot do it daily, then every other day will still yield results. The idea is to do it regularly.

**2. Keep studying the 12 Steps.** I recommend studying the 12 Steps with your mentor, and members of your sangha. This will keep everyone engaged.

**3. Stay involved in your sangha.** By having a commitment to others, you will be surrounded by other members who are just as serious about their practice as you are.

**4. Share the gift of mindfulness meditation.** By mentoring and recruiting other members, you will be helping them find freedom from their suffering. They will be forever grateful to you for your help.

**5.  Attend a mindfulness meditation retreat.** Once you experience the full power of the retreat, you will realize just how much it can help you realize your true potential as a human and spiritual being. In order to achieve the greatest personal transformation, I recommend at least a 5-7 day retreat.

# Letter to the Reader

Dear Reader,

Thank you for staying with me this far. I hope this is the beginning of our spiritual journey together. As you travel the path to inner peace, you will discover many wonderful things about yourself that you never imagined. You are now a mindful leader, and have the power to inspire others. You are now a shining example for your peers to follow.

Here at the Mindfulness Meditation Institute, Mary and I are working hard to develop new tools to help you succeed in your practice. Some of our future projects include: mindfulness meditation retreats, a book on advanced level practice, a book on building the mindful organization, and much more. We look forward to making these available to you as soon as possible.

We're excited about the recognition mindfulness meditation is getting in the mainstream media. It recently made the cover of Time magazine, and marketing firms are calling it one of the top trends in 2014 and beyond. These are clear indications that the practice is compatible with Western values, so its popularity will only continue growing.

Remember, it doesn't matter at what age you begin your spiritual journey. The most important time in your life is the present moment. What matters most is what you do now. All it takes is one very mindful breath to touch nirvana, and realize freedom from your suffering.

I want to thank you for allowing me to be your teacher in the practice of mindfulness meditation. It has been an honor and a privilege to be a part of your life. I hope that we'll have the opportunity to meet in person in the near future, so we can walk this path together. In the meantime, keep up the good work. And remember, together we can make world peace a reality, and not just a cliché.

Warmest regards,

Charles A. Francis

P.S. I would love to hear about your successes (or challenges) with the practice, so feel free to email me at Charles@MindfulnessMeditationInstitute.org.

# Appendix

# The 12 Steps of the Mindfulness Meditation Practice

Personal fulfillment is available to anyone willing to put in the effort to pursue it. Through the practice of mindfulness meditation, we can transform our lives and relationships for greater peace and harmony. These are the steps we followed in order to achieve freedom from our suffering. By dwelling in the three main sources of spiritual nourishment: our True Nature, the spiritual principles, and our spiritual community, we learned to live mindfully in the present moment.

1. We became aware of the pain and suffering created by unmindful thoughts, speech, and actions.

2. We learned how to develop our primary tools of observation: concentration and mindfulness.

3. We sought to eliminate the things that agitate our mind, and prevent us from achieving inner peace and serenity.

4. We learned how to structure our meditation session for maximum effectiveness, and to fit our lifestyle.

5. In order to ensure our spiritual development, we made mindfulness meditation a regular practice.

6. We remained vigilant in our meditation practice, so that we continued making steady progress.

7. We became aware that other people can provide us with the spiritual nourishment vital to our development.

8. We sought to cultivate peace and harmony in our relationships and interactions with others by practicing deep listening, mindful speech, non-judging, and forgiveness.

9. We sought to dwell deeply in our spiritual community in order to enhance our development, and that of others.

10. We became aware of how unmindful consumption perpetuates our suffering, and prevents us from achieving true inner peace.

11. With the strength, courage, and mindfulness we attained through our meditation practice, we confronted and overcame the wounds from our past.

12. Having found freedom from our suffering through mindfulness meditation, we shared this practice with others, and continued dwelling deeply in the present moment through mindful living.

## Meditation Goal Statement Exercise

If you're serious about your meditation practice, then you'll make the commitment to practicing diligently. A goal statement is a powerful tool to help you stay on track. This exercise will make it easy for you to prepare your statement, and show you how to use it for maximum effectiveness.

I have included a sample format. You can either simply fill in the blanks, or use it as a model for your own statement. The two most important elements of a meditation goal statement are: (1) what you will do, and (2) how long you will do it. Here are my suggestions for a successful meditation practice:

- **Practice sitting meditation regularly.** I recommend a minimum of twenty minutes per day to start. I suggest increasing the duration as you become able to sit longer. Use the meditation techniques outlined on our website, or in the *Quick Start to Mindfulness Meditation* CD.

- **Practice writing meditation regularly.** I would recommend at least ten minutes per day. Include your goal statement as part of the writing meditation. You can do this at any time of the day, though you'll probably see better results if you do it right before your sitting meditation session.

- **Attend a mindfulness meditation meeting regularly.** Meditating with others is essential to your spiritual development. I recommend attending at least one meeting per week, and that you get actively involved in the group.

If none of the meetings in your area focus on good mindfulness meditation techniques, then I recommend you start your own group. Our group starter kit makes this easy for you. You can download it from the Resources page of our website.

I should caution you to not make your goals overly ambitious. Otherwise, you'll never achieve them, and you'll get discouraged and quit. Make your goals realistically achievable, taking into consideration your commitments. Remember, you can revise them at any time.

Also, don't get upset if you have a minor lapse in your routine. Don't worry if you miss a day or two of practicing. Just do your best to stick to your goals. Here is a sample goal statement you can use. Simply fill in the blanks with the necessary information:

### "My Meditation Goal Statement"

*"I,_____(your name)_____, realize that through a diligent mindfulness meditation practice, I will see an immediate and continuous spiritual transformation in myself.*

*For the next_____(period of time, e.g. month)_____, I commit to practicing mindfulness meditation regularly. I will practice writing meditation for at least____minutes per day. I will practice sitting meditation for at least____minutes per day. I will also attend a mindfulness meditation meeting every_____."*

Remember to include this goal statement as part of your regular writing meditation exercise. In other words, copy your goal statement every time you do the exercise. This is a powerful way of imprinting it in your subconscious, making it much more likely that you will follow through on your goals.

I would also suggest you post your goal statement some place where you'll see it often, such as the wall by your desk. This will help remind you of your commitment to yourself.

Once you have achieved these goals, establish new goals and revise your statement accordingly. You may want to increase the amount of time and/or frequency of each element.

At any time, you may decide that you want to establish some unique goals in your practice. For example, if you decide to start a mindfulness meditation meeting in your area, include that in your revised goal statement.

Remember, the purpose of your goal statement is to help you stay committed to your meditation practice, so that you keep progressing in your spiritual development.

## Writing Meditations

### Instructions

The following writing meditations will help you tremendously in your mindfulness meditation practice. They will reprogram your subconscious to change your thinking and behavior without any conscious effort. Choose the one that applies the most to your specific needs and current level of practice.

The loving-kindness meditation will help you transform your relationships by enabling you to be more kind and loving. It will help you heal the wounds from your past, as you become more forgiving and understanding. It will also speed up your spiritual development, because you'll be able to connect with people on a deeper level. This will provide you with the spiritual nourishment you need to grow.

Simply copy the verses by hand in a notebook or journal, every day for about 10-15 minutes. Any time of the day is fine, and you don't necessarily need a quiet place. It doesn't matter how far you get each time.

Simply write for a few minutes every day. Then the next day, pick up where you left off.

## Loving-Kindness Writing Meditation

### Yourself

May I be healthy and strong. May I be safe and protected. May I be peaceful and free from mental, emotional, and physical suffering. May I be happy and joyful. May I be patient and understanding. May I be loving, kind, compassionate, and gentle in my ways. May I be courageous in dealing with difficulties, and always meet with success. May I be diligent and committed to my spiritual practice, and to helping others along their path. May my True Nature shine through, and onto all beings I encounter.

### Everyone in Your House

May every person and living being in my house be healthy and strong. May they be safe and protected. May they be peaceful and free from mental, emotional, and physical suffering. May they be happy and joyful. May they be patient and understanding. May they be loving, kind, compassionate, and gentle in their ways. May they be courageous in dealing with difficulties, and always meet with success. May they be diligent and committed to their spiritual practice, and to helping others along their path. May their True Nature shine through, and onto all beings they encounter.

### Your Neighborhood

May every person and living being in my neighborhood be healthy and strong. May they be safe and protected. May they be peaceful and free from mental, emotional, and physical suffering. May they be happy and joyful. May they be patient and understanding. May they be loving, kind, compassionate, and gentle in their ways. May they be courageous in dealing with difficulties, and always meet with success. May they be diligent and committed to their spiritual practice, and to helping others along their path. May their True Nature shine through, and onto all beings they encounter.

## Your City

May every person and living being in my city be healthy and strong. May they be safe and protected. May they be peaceful and free from mental, emotional, and physical suffering. May they be happy and joyful. May they be patient and understanding. May they be loving, kind, compassionate, and gentle in their ways. May they be courageous in dealing with difficulties, and always meet with success. May they be diligent and committed to their spiritual practice, and to helping others along their path. May their True Nature shine through, and onto all beings they encounter.

## Your Country

May every person and living being in my country be healthy and strong. May they be safe and protected. May they be peaceful and free from mental, emotional, and physical suffering. May they be happy and joyful. May they be patient and understanding. May they be loving, kind, compassionate, and gentle in their ways. May they be courageous in dealing with difficulties, and always meet with success. May they be diligent and committed to their spiritual practice, and to helping others along their path. May their True Nature shine through, and onto all beings they encounter.

## The Whole Planet

May every person and living being on earth be healthy and strong. May they be safe and protected. May they be peaceful and free from mental, emotional, and physical suffering. May they be happy and joyful. May they be patient and understanding. May they be loving, kind, compassionate, and gentle in their ways. May they be courageous in dealing with difficulties, and always meet with success. May they be diligent and committed to their spiritual practice, and to helping others along their path. May their True Nature shine through, and onto all beings they encounter.

## The Entire Universe

May every person and living being in the entire universe on all planes of existence be healthy and strong. May they be safe and protected. May they be peaceful and free from mental, emotional, and physical suffering. May they be happy and joyful. May they be patient and understanding. May they be loving, kind, compassionate, and gentle in their ways. May they be courageous in dealing with difficulties, and always meet with success. May they be diligent and committed to their spiritual practice, and to helping others along their path. May their True Nature shine through, and onto all beings they encounter.

## Mindful Consumption Writing Meditation

As I continue practicing mindfulness meditation, I am becoming an enlightened being, and a more mindful consumer. There is a beautiful person within me wanting to emerge. May I be loving, kind, and compassionate with myself and allow this wonderful person to shine through, and see him/her each time I look into the mirror. May I be aware of the thousands of other people just like me who are walking the same spiritual path.

May I live deeply in the present moment and be aware of the messages my body is sending me. May I be aware of the unconscious environmental triggers that influence my consumption. May I learn which foods and nutrients nourish my body and mind, and lead to optimal health, performance, and longevity—and not simply a number on a weight scale. May I realize that there is no right or wrong in dieting—only mindfulness. I will rejoice in my successes, and will not feel guilt, shame, or remorse over minor lapses.

Being a mindful consumer, may I eat the foods and nutrients that will promote good health, longevity, and mindfulness. May I incorporate sufficient physical activity into my daily routine wherever possible to promote physical, mental, and emotional well-being. May I be mindful of substances such as alcohol, tobacco, unnecessary medications, and other substances that are robbing me of my spiritual growth, and have the courage to let them go. May I continue to be diligent and committed to my spiritual practice, and to helping others along their path, so that we may all find inner peace. May my True Nature shine through and onto everyone I encounter.

## Living the Mindfulness Meditation Practice Writing Meditation

### The Mindfulness Revolution

I realize that I am living in a wonderful and exciting time in history—the age of the Mindfulness Revolution. I am part of a movement in which millions of people are changing the world through the practice of mindfulness meditation. Through this simple and effective practice, we are transforming our lives to attain inner peace, wisdom, and good health—without having to abandon our spiritual roots. I am aware that the practice can also heal the wounds in my society to bring about peace, harmony, and goodwill. As a pioneer in this thriving movement, I will work with other spiritual seekers to share the gift of mindfulness meditation to make peace on earth a reality.

### My Spiritual Goals

I realize that through diligent mindfulness meditation practice, I will see an immediate transformation in myself. As a spiritual seeker walking the path to inner peace, may I be determined and committed to my daily meditation practice, as well as writing meditation, so that I continue making steady progress. May I persevere to continue learning about the practice, so that I can be a teacher, a role model, and a leader for others to follow. May I dwell deeply in the three sources of spiritual nourishment: my True Nature, the spiritual principles, and my spiritual community, so that I enhance my spiritual development and shorten my path to enlightenment.

## My Meditation Practice

May I work to reduce the unnecessary agitation of my mind, so that my practice is easier and more productive. May I work to develop concentration and mindfulness during each meditation session, so that I may see the world with clarity and wisdom, and gain a deeper understanding of the true nature of my existence. May I confront the wounds from my past with courage and determination, so that I eliminate them as obstacles to my practice and continue growing. May I cultivate deeper connections with everyone I encounter, so that we freely share the energy of mindfulness, and enhance each other's spiritual development.

## Loving-Kindness in My Relationships

I realize that mindfulness is a way of life for cultivating peace and harmony in all my relationships. May I learn to live deeply in the present moment by practicing mindful breathing, mindful walking, deep listening, and mindful speech in all my affairs. May I be patient and understanding, forgiving and compassionate with everyone I encounter throughout my day. May I be loving, kind, and gentle in my ways. May I be courageous in dealing with difficulties, and always meet with success.

## Mindful Consumption in My Personal Life

As I continue to practice mindfulness meditation, I am becoming an enlightened being and a more mindful consumer. May I consume the foods and nutrients that will promote good health, longevity, and mindfulness. May I engage in sufficient daily physical activity wherever possible, to promote physical, mental, and emotional well-being.

May I be mindful of the consumption of alcohol, tobacco, unnecessary medications, and other substances that are depriving me of my spiritual growth—and have the willingness, courage, and strength to let them go.

## Mindful Consumption in My Community

As I continue to practice mindfulness meditation, I am developing greater awareness of the interdependent nature of all the systems in the world, and how my actions affect my community and the environment. May I be a mindful consumer of resources in all my activities, and work toward contributing to the long-term viability of the human race.

May I consume natural resources such as water, plants, and minerals in moderation so that I contribute to peace and harmony among different societies, and preserve the resources for future generations. May I work with others to promote the efficient use of resources at work, so that I help my organization become a good corporate citizen. I know that by advocating mindful consumption, I am making a great contribution to my community.

## Carrying the Message

I am grateful for the gift of inner peace I have received through the practice of mindfulness meditation. As I continue to practice, I am becoming a messenger of peace and harmony. My compassion for other people's suffering is awakening my sense of duty to help them find this gift. I realize that in order to keep what I have, I need to share it with others.

May I carry the message of inner peace to others by sharing my experience with the mindfulness meditation practice, and how it has transformed my life and relationships. I realize that by sharing the gift of inner peace, I will find true joy and fulfillment, knowing that I have made a tremendous difference in someone else's life. Even if I help just one person to begin the path to spiritual freedom, I know I have made a great contribution to my community.

## Building My Spiritual Community

As I am aware that my spiritual community is essential for my ongoing personal development, may I work to build a strong and healthy meditation group. May I help recruit new members, so that they too can learn how to practice mindfulness meditation, and walk the path to inner peace. May I be a good role model and mentor to help guide them in their practice. May I help my meditation group stay focused on its core mission of teaching mindfulness meditation, so that it becomes a spiritual refuge for everyone who needs healing and peace of mind. I know that by building a strong and healthy meditation group, I am making an important contribution to my community, and society as a whole.

## The 5 Suggestions of the Mindfulness Meditation Practice

Our experience has shown that we can make significant progress in our spiritual development through mindfulness meditation. Here is a formula we've found to help meditators get the most from their practice:

1. Practice sitting and writing meditation daily.
2. Attend at least 1 meditation meeting per week.
3. Find a mentor who can guide you through the practice.
4. Work the 12 Steps of the Mindfulness Meditation Practice.
5. Get involved in your meditation group.

These suggestions are designed to connect us with the 3 main sources of our spiritual nourishment: our True Nature, the spiritual principles, and our spiritual community.

# Glossary

**attachment.** A mental or emotional clinging to an object we believe will bring us happiness, security, or emotional gratification. We often cling to things such as material possessions, people, and views.

**aversion.** A strong dislike toward something we find unpleasant to our senses or emotions, such as a person, place, or memory. Our natural inclination is to avoid the object.

**Buddha.** The title given to a person who has achieved enlightenment. It also refers to Siddhartha Gautama, the founder of Buddhism, after he achieved his enlightenment.

**Buddha Nature.** The Buddhist term describing the conscious essence of who we really are; also referred to as our True Nature, higher consciousness, or spirit. It is one of the Three Jewels.

**compassion.** A sympathetic concern for the well-being or suffering of others; not to be confused with emotional sensitivity, which is an ego-centric concern for one's own feelings.

**concentration.** The act of focusing our attention on an object without being distracted by other internal or external objects.

**conditioned response.** An automatic response developed through repeated exposure to a stimulus.

**deep listening.** The practice of using concentration and compassion to listen to others when they are speaking to us. Listening with sincere interest.

**Dharma.** The spiritual principles that govern our existence. The teachings of the Buddha to explain the universal spiritual laws as they apply to human suffering. It is one of the Three Jewels.

**ego.** A person's sense of self, or personal identity.

**emotional sensitivity.** A person's ego-centric concern for his own feelings; not to be confused with compassion, which is a concern for another's well-being. An emotionally sensitive person has his feelings hurt easily.

**enlightenment.** The state of having become spiritually awakened. Having the ability to see the true nature of reality without views or emotions altering one's perceptions.

**epiphany.** A moment of sudden insight or revelation. A breakthrough in one's spiritual development.

**Five Hindrances.** In Buddhism, these are the five mental states that prevent us from achieving mindfulness. They are sensual desire, aversion, lethargy, agitation, and doubt.

**Four Establishments of Mindfulness.** In Buddhism, these are the four practices by which we attain mindfulness. They are mindfulness of the body, feelings, consciousness, and phenomena or objects of the mind.

**Four Noble Truths.** The Buddha's teaching on the nature of suffering. They are: (1) the existence of suffering, (2) the origins of suffering, (3) the cessation of suffering, and (4) the path that leads to the cessation of suffering. They are the foundation of Buddhism.

**impermanence.** The idea that everything in the universe is temporary, and always changing. Nothing remains the same. Much of our suffering arises when we cling to things that are temporary.

**interconnectedness.** The worldview that sees that everything is part of a greater whole. It implies that we depend on each other for our existence.

**lethargy.** A mental dullness; lack of energy and enthusiasm. It manifests itself into boredom and/or drowsiness.

**loving-kindness.** Unconditional love for all living beings. There are no expectations of receiving anything in return for our acts of kindness.

**loving-kindness meditation.** A traditional Buddhist form of meditation whereby practitioners read, recite, or listen to a set of affirmations in order to reinforce unconditional love for all living beings.

**mental agitation.** The over-stimulation of our mind; usually the result of being involved in too many activities, too much background noise, or unresolved painful memories.

**mental discipline.** The ability to control one's own mind through concentration, mindfulness, and inner strength.

**mental formations.** A network of thought patterns that make up our views and beliefs. They determine our actions, including conditioned responses.

**mentor.** A person who acts as a guide in the practice of mindfulness meditation.

**mindful consumption.** The consumption of nutrients and resources (natural and man-made) in a way that is not wasteful, so that we do not put undue strain on our body, community, or fragile societies. Examples would be mindful eating for good health, conservation of natural resources, and frugal use of financial resources.

**mindful leadership.** Leading people and making decisions about the use of resources in a way that maximizes productivity, peace, and harmony. A mindful leader is aware of the long-term implications of his actions, and that of his followers, and works toward environmental, economic, and social sustainability.

**mindfulness.** Awareness of the nature of our existence, and our relationship to others and the rest of the world. With mindfulness we can make decisions on how to minimize suffering, and maximize peace for ourselves and those around us.

**mindfulness energy.** The energy of consciousness that enables us to see with greater clarity, so that we can make better decisions. It enables us to build inner strength.

**mindfulness meditation.** The form of quiet reflection that enables us to develop mental discipline and insight into the true nature of our existence, and our relationship to others and the rest of the world. The goal is to achieve freedom from suffering.

**nirvana.** The state of complete awareness and freedom from suffering, desire, and sense of separate self. It is oneness with the universe.

**Noble Eightfold Path.** The teaching of the Buddha that outlines the path to freedom from suffering; (1) right view, (2) right thinking, (3) right speech, (4) right action, (5) right livelihood, (6) right effort, (7) right mindfulness, and (8) right concentration.

**noble silence.** A period of deep silence practiced during spiritual retreats in order to help calm the mind, and facilitate personal reflection.

**power struggle.** A competition for control in interpersonal relationships and interactions. The goal is to gain the upper hand by getting people to accept one's views, and to make them unsure of themselves.

**Sangha.** The spiritual community that supports our practice. It generally refers to the meditation group where we practice with others. It is one of the sources of spiritual nourishment, that is, one of the Three Jewels.

**sensual desire.** The wanting to please our five senses: sight, sound, smell, taste, and touch. It is one of the Five Hindrances that keeps us from developing mindfulness.

**Siddhartha Gautama.** The young prince who lived in northern India 2,500 years ago who achieved enlightenment through meditation. After his enlightenment, he became known as the Buddha, "The Awakened One."

**spiritual awakening.** An experience where a person attains a higher level of consciousness. It is usually marked by a deep sense of peace and interconnectedness with the universe. Some of the effects can be permanent, while others subside.

**spiritual evolution.** The process of gradually awakening our higher consciousness. It usually comes through some form of spiritual practice.

**suffering.** Ongoing physical, mental, or emotional pain. See also Four Noble Truths.

**system.** In general, a group of components working toward a goal, such as a nation, economy, or ecosystem. Everything is part of a system, and all systems are part of a broader system.

**systems evolution.** The process by which a system achieves its primary goal(s) in an increasingly more efficient and effective manner. This usually involves increasing levels of complexity and self-awareness in how a system processes inputs to convert them into outputs.

**Theravada Buddhism.** The oldest branch of Buddhism. It emphasizes the individual's meditation practice as the means to enlightenment. Its doctrine states that insight comes through the practitioner's experience, use of knowledge, and critical reasoning.

**Three Jewels.** The Buddha, the Dharma, and the Sangha. These are the sources of mindfulness energy—the spiritual nourishment necessary to develop mindfulness, so we can see reality with greater clarity.

**True Nature.** See Buddha Nature.

**unconditional love.** The ideal form of love where we help others without expectation of receiving anything in return. We give simply out of compassion for the suffering of other living beings.

**validation.** The affirmation of the worth of a person's feelings or opinions, which are elements of the ego.

**worry.** To give way to anxiety and unease, and allow one's mind to dwell on difficulties or troubles. It is usually founded on unrealistic thinking.

**writing meditation.** The repetitive writing of positive affirmations in order to reprogram one's subconscious. This form of writing meditation was developed by the Mindfulness Meditation Institute.

# Index